Contract Costing for Union Negotiators

Contract Costing for Union Negotiators

By Donald Spatz

Union Communication Services, Inc.
Annapolis, MD

Unionist.com

Copyright © 2009 by Donald Spatz. All rights reserved.

No part of this book may be photocopied or reproduced in any other manner whatsoever without written permission. For permission information or to purchase additional copies, address UCS, Inc., 165 Conduit Street, Annapolis, Maryland 21401; phone 410-626-1400; e-mail ucs@unionist.com. Visit us on the Web at unionist.com.

Library of Congress Control Number: 2009939448

ISBN-13: 978-0-9659486-7-8

ISBN-10: 0-9659486-7-6

Union Communication Services, Inc., is a union shop, whose employees are members of Local 400, United Food and Commercial Workers.

Printed and bound in the United States of America by PPMW/CWA members at Doyle Printing & Offset Company, Inc., Landover, MD.

0 9 8 7 6 5 4 3

First Edition

Table of Contents

Introduction 1
Chapter 1– Basic Concepts for Costing a Union Contract 6
    Total Annual Cost 6
    Average Annual Cost per Employee 6
    Average Cost per Employee per Hour 7
    Requesting Data from the Employer 7
    The Employer's Duty to Provide Information 8
Chapter 2 – Wages and Salaries (without step progression) 11
    FORMAT WORKSHEET #1 11
        Data from the Regional Medical Center (RMC) 13
    What about Probationary Employees? 20
Chapter 3 – Wages and Salaries (with step progression) 21
    FORMAT WORKSHEET #2 21
        Data from the Regional Medical Center 22
    A Few More Points on Calculating Average Straight-Time Wages 25
Chapter 4 – Productive Hours 27
    FORMAT WORKSHEET #3 27
        Data from the Regional Medical Center 28
Chapter 5 – Hourly Wage-Related Premium Payments 31
    FORMAT WORKSHEET #4 31
    Overtime Premiums 31
        Data from the Regional Medical Center 32
    Shift Differentials 33
        Data from the Regional Medical Center 35
    Other Hourly Wage Premiums 36
    Skill-Based Hourly Premiums 37
        Data from the Regional Medical Center 37
Chapter 6 – Pay for Non-Work Time 39
    Holidays 39
    FORMAT WORKSHEET #5 40
        Data from the Regional Medical Center 40
    Personal Days 41
        Data from the Regional Medical Center 41
    Sick Leave 42
        Data from the Regional Medical Center 42
    Bereavement Leaves, Jury Duty Leaves and Leaves for Union Business 43
    Severance Pay 43
Chapter 7 – Vacations 44
    FORMAT WORKSHEET #6 44

  Data from the Regional Medical Center..46
Chapter 8 – Health/Dental/Life/Disability Insurance 48
 Health Insurance...48
 FORMAT WORKSHEET #7..48
  Data from the Regional Medical Center..50
 Dental Insurance...51
  Data from the Regional Medical Center..52
 Life Insurance..53
 Short-Term Disability/Sickness and Accident Benefits..54
  Data from the Regional Medical Center..55
 Other Insurance Coverage...55
Chapter 9 – Annual Payments and Allowances..56
 Retirement Plans...56
 Supplemental Unemployment Benefits...56
 FORMAT WORKSHEET #8..57
  Data from the Regional Medical Center..58
Chapter 10 – Summary of Contractual Costs and Roll-Up......................................60
 FORMAT WORKSHEET #9..60
 Roll-Up..61
  RMC Summary and Roll-up Factor...63
Chapter 11 – Using the Workbook in Negotiations 64
 The Medical Center Negotiations..64
 Union Proposal #1...65
  Increment Increase and Percent Wage Increase...65
  Holidays and Personal Days..68
  Vacations...70
  Health Insurance..72
  Longevity Annual Bonus..73
  Summary of Union Proposal #1...74
 Regional Medical Center Proposal #1...75
  Flat Wage Increase and Increment Increase..76
  Health Insurance..78
  Shift Differentials...80
  Vacations...82
  Summary of Regional Medical Center Proposal #1..83
 Union Proposal #2...84
 Regional Medical Center Proposal #2...87
 The Final Agreement..90
 A Last Point..91
Appendix...92
Index..94
Acknowledgements..98
About the author..98

Introduction

A UNION NEGOTIATING committee will make many judgments during the course of negotiations with its employer. Some of those decisions involve evaluating the value of its own proposals and comparing them with offers made by the employer. Others involve comparison of various alternatives in union caucuses – determining which proposal would provide maximum benefit to the bargaining unit. As negotiations move toward the endpoint, the committee will be making decisions in a pressure-filled environment. By having accurate data available on the wage structure and various other benefits of the current contract and by preparing and regularly updating estimates of the value (costs) of the union's and the employer's proposals, the union negotiating committee will be in a good position to make its decisions in the most expeditious, thoughtful and careful way.

Costing a labor agreement is not an exact or perfect science. Obviously, mathematical formulas are used to make calculations. But these calculations are based on the availability of underlying data and, in many cases, some assumptions. Costing a bargaining unit's current contract should be viewed as taking a 'snap-shot in time'. The calculations that the negotiating committee makes to determine the average straight-time (base) wage, the value of various contractual benefits, such as overtime premiums, pay for time not worked, health insurance and other types of fringe benefits will be based on a certain time period – the point at which the committee is assembling and analyzing the underlying data in preparation for negotiations.

The workplace is not static. Senior employees retire; new employees are hired; employees are eligible for an additional week of vacation; an employee takes paid bereavement or jury duty leave. All these events will change the cost to an employer and the benefit to the union and its members. So the 'snap-shot in time', which is as accurate as possible for the point in time in which it is taken, should be viewed only as an estimate of the benefits (costs). Still, using this accurate snap-shot, the union negotiating committee can make more knowledgeable decisions during the course of negotiations and will better know how those decisions will affect the overall bargaining unit and subgroups of members.

Accurate benefit (cost) information is essential to the union negotiating committee for several reasons:

1. To help make decisions as to which proposals or counterproposals will best meet the needs of union members while preparing for and conducting negotiations.
2. To check the validity of employer statements about the costs of its proposals (and the union's proposals) at the negotiating table.
3. To evaluate the total economic welfare or value of the contract and to examine and compare its various components, understanding that various 'trade-offs' have been made in previous contracts and that during the course of the current negotiations the union committee will need to do so again,

using the best possible information to do so.
4. To be able to thoroughly explain to the union members the economic outcome of negotiations and why the union negotiating committee made the decisions it did.

This manual cannot review in detail every possible type of union contract because there are so many different industries, employees and contractual benefits covered by collective agreements. In some cases employees are paid monthly salaries; in others, weekly salaries are the norm; and in still others a considerable portion of weekly earnings might come from incentive plans (either individual or group-based). Yet for many union contracts, an hourly wage is the norm and this manual focuses primarily on costing a collective agreement covering employees who are paid on an hourly basis.

Fringe benefits are almost limitless in their variety and in their application among various industry sectors and collective agreements. For that reason, this manual covers those that are most common across many union contracts and seeks to explain the fundamental concepts of evaluating the benefits (costs) of fringe benefits so that union negotiators can adapt the concepts to their own particular circumstances.

Chapter 1 reviews the three basic formats in which contract costing data is assembled and discusses the union's right to request and receive information from the employer in order to bargain intelligently. Understanding these three formats and requesting salient information from the employer is one of the first tasks for the union committee. After obtaining the best and most accurate data upon which to cost the contract the committee is better able to analyze members' ideas, prepare solid initial proposals and understand the impact of counter proposals or modified proposals developed by either party at the negotiating table.

Each subsequent chapter of the manual reviews various categories of common contractual benefits (costs), starting with wages in Chapters 2 and 3.

Chapter 2 covers the calculation of an average straight-time (base) wage rate for a bargaining unit with established job classifications or wage classifications that encompass multiple job categories without 'progression' or 'steps' within individual job or wage classifications.

Chapter 3 adds methodology to incorporate progression or steps within each job or wage classification based on years of service or other criteria specified in the contract.

Chapter 4 discusses the concept of 'productive hours' as the basis for expressing the value of various contractual benefits in the format of Average Cost per Employee per Hour.

Chapter 5 reviews various kinds of premium payments related to hours actually worked such as overtime pay, shift differentials, premium payments for unscheduled hours, work on holidays or weekends or 6th or 7th consecutive days or premiums based on extra skill, education or job responsibilities.

Chapter 6 examines contractual obligations of the employer to pay wages for 'non-work time', most often holidays, vacations, personal days, sick leave and other kinds of leave, for instance for bereavement, serving on a jury, education or training courses or conducting union business. Severance pay could be considered to fall into this category as could supplemental unemployment benefits (SUB). However, the latter has been incorporated into Chapter 9.

Chapter 7 provides a methodology for calculating the cost of annual vacations and how to link the categories of vacation eligibility to a seniority list.

Chapter 8 shows how to cost various types of insurance benefits: health insurance, dental insurance, life insurance and disability insurance covering short-term sickness or injury.

Chapter 9 covers contractual benefits that are paid on an annual basis or on some other less-than-regular time period. Here pension plans as well as the SUB plans are reviewed as well as benefits such as tuition reimbursement, clothing or tool allowances, and longevity bonuses paid after employees have reached the top of their progression.

Chapter 10 explains how the union negotiating committee can pull all the costing information together into one comprehensive summary document and discusses the concept of 'roll-up' cost, sometimes called the 'multiplier'.

Chapter 11 shows how this 'baseline' costing information can be used to estimate the costs of a union's initial bargaining proposals, how to do the same with an employer's initial proposal and, in essence, how to use costing techniques during the course of negotiations.

The Appendix has a sample letter to an employer to request information for collective bargaining.

The manual does not discuss legally-mandated contributions by an employer, for example payments for Social Security and Medicare (FICA) or contributions to State-based Unemployment Compensation or Workers' Compensation. Though these payments are certainly a cost for the employer they are not negotiated as part of the collective bargaining process and all employers are required to make these contributions. There is no need to cover them in this manual.

I participated in my first contract negotiations in 1973, serving primarily as a 'technician' on the union side of the table. It was my responsibility to watch the details of the negotiations, both the numbers as well as contract language. My recollection is that 'hand-held', albeit rather large, electronic calculators were available then. While it sure beat long-hand multiplication, division, addition and subtraction it was a far cry from the possibilities available with PCs today.

As PCs and spreadsheet software became more readily available, many employers became much more sophisticated not only in payroll and cost-accounting methods but also at the negotiating table. Certainly some unions managed to follow the trend and developed spreadsheets to help them manage their side of the negotiating table. Yet it is true that too often unions did not avail themselves of these technologies.

While teaching contract negotiations at the AFL-CIO's George Meany Center for Labor Studies/National Labor College during much of the 1990s, the class sessions on contract costing were still conducted using hand-held calculators – mainly for lack of appropriate computing facilities. Thankfully, that is now changed.

This manual is an outgrowth of a short training program initially prepared for the American Federation of Teachers' (AFT) Health Care Division in 2003 at which time it was abundantly clear that the fundamentals of using Microsoft Excel software to build spreadsheets should be incorporated into training for union negotiators on the basic concepts of contract costing.

This manual has twin goals: explaining in some detail the fundamentals of costing a union collective bargaining agreement; and building the confidence of union negotiators to prepare their own MS Excel workbooks to help them at the negotiating table. I do not consider myself an expert on using every aspect of MS Excel, in large part because there are so many sophisticated features. Indeed, for me it was a matter of self-learning with some help from a basic Microsoft book, Mastering Microsoft Office 97, regularly using the Help function in Excel and, of course, by simply experimenting. And I had the opportunity to learn many new tips and tricks from more knowledgeable students in subsequent training programs.

This book is accompanied with a CD containing several Excel workbooks prepared using Microsoft Excel 2007 and saved so they are compatible with Microsoft Excel 1997-2003. The FORMAT FOLDER has two workbooks: the 'Format Workbook' contains nine worksheet templates with pre-entered formulas that can be used by the reader to develop his or her own worksheets, following the suggestions in this manual and modifying the worksheets to fit the particular circumstances of his or her own collective agreement. The 'Blank Workbook' has the text formats for the nine worksheets but has no pre-entered formulas.

The RMC FOLDER has a 'RMC Workbook' that fully costs a contract following the basic templates of the Format Workbook. The RMC Workbook has a tenth worksheet named Data from Employer containing information on wages and benefits for a simulated contract (Regional Medical Center) based on a compilation of several collective agreements negotiated by the AFT Health Care Division. The data have been modified for the purpose of illustrating as many kinds of contractual benefits as possible while using realistic data but should not be considered representative of any one contract.

There are four additional workbooks named Union Proposal #1, RMC Proposal #1, Union Proposal #2 and RMC Proposal #2 which follow the course of negotiating sessions, costing the proposals exchanged between the parties as well as their final agreement. The methods used in these workbooks are described in Chapter 11. The sample information request letter in the Appendix is also on the CD in Word format.

None of the workbooks are 'protected'. Column and row headings and formulas as well as the data and calculated costs can be deleted or modified by the reader. This also means that the original files cannot be reconstructed if they are deleted unintentionally. It is the choice of the reader whether backup copies of any or all of the workbooks are made.

Unfortunately, there is no one union contract that could serve as the 'best' model for the purpose of learning the fundamentals of contract costing. The reader is obliged to modify, expand upon and even ignore some of the templates or formats in these pre-prepared worksheets so that they are useful and relevant for his or her own collective bargaining agreement. It is my hope that the explanations and examples given here are sufficiently clear to permit the reader to do so.

Likewise, it is impossible to fully cover every detail or nuance of how to use Microsoft Excel to build spreadsheets for contract costing purposes. It will require some experimentation and self-learning on your part. Using some of the learning aids prepared by Microsoft or other authors specifically on Excel or MS Office also could be very useful to the reader. **Though MS Excel 97-2003 and MS Excel 2007 perform essentially the same functions, the older version will not open files prepared in the newer version. For that reason, the CD contains both file formats. Please choose the correct folder for your version of Excel software.**

The 'look' of MS Excel 2007 is vastly different from its earlier version, especially in its Toolbar ribbon. For that reason, it made little sense to make screen images of the toolbars in either the newer or the older version of the program. Although there are no pictures of the toolbar functions, the steps that are taken to enter formulas, format cells, copy, paste and other functions are described as completely as possible. Readers will need to become familiar with the exact location of these tools in the MS Excel 97-2003 software or in the MS Excel 2007 software. Readers using operating systems other than Windows (e.g., MAC-OS, Linux) may find that instructions for executing certain Excel functions are slightly different.

Like most manuals, it makes sense to go through Contract Costing for Union Negotiators from the beginning, as many concepts and Excel instructions in later chapters assume knowledge of techniques from earlier chapters. Most of the fundamentals of Excel are covered in Chapter 2 and readers who feel comfortable with using the software program can skip quickly through the 'Excel Basics' boxes. The index should guide the reader to appropriate text when there is a need to search for a specific issue.

A final introductory note: union negotiating committees should use contract costing as a tool to assist in their decision-making, not as a substitute for thoughtfulness on the part of the entire committee. Committee members need to nurture good listening skills within their own committee and across the negotiating table. Committee members need to look for the best and most reasonable compromises (again, within their own committee and across the negotiating table). And union negotiators must always remember that certain principles and values for workers cannot always be captured in just dollars and cents.

Chapter 1– Basic Concepts for Costing a Union Contract

THE COSTS OF NEGOTIATED wage or salary scales plus other contractually negotiated benefits can be expressed in a number of different ways. The three most common, which are inter-related, are:

1. Total Annual Cost
2. Average Annual Cost per Employee
3. Average Cost per Employee per Hour

Total Annual Cost

Total Annual Cost is the cost to the employer for a certain contractual benefit for a contract year or calendar/fiscal year. It is often the most valuable and straight-forward way to express the cost to the employer (and the monetary value to the members of the bargaining unit) of a provision in the contract.

For some types of contractual benefits that can be highly variable in their usage (for instance. bereavement leave or tuition reimbursement), the most logical way to assemble the information is by asking the employer to add up the total amount that it paid in a contract or calendar year for that particular item. Indeed, most employers will have special cost-accounting codes to capture this information during routine payroll processing. For these variable types of contractual benefits, it often makes sense to ask for and maintain data over several years since the cost can differ considerably from one year to the next, depending on the size of the bargaining unit and their experience in using a benefit in a particular year. While these are often not significant costs to an employer they are a highly-valued benefit when, for instance, an employee must travel or make arrangements for a loved one's funeral.

Average Annual Cost per Employee

The second way of expressing costs, Average Annual Cost per Employee, is simply the Total Annual Cost divided by the number of employees in the bargaining unit. Of course, that latter number is not usually static over the course of a year. New employees are hired; some employees retire or otherwise leave employment. So, in calculating the Average Annual Cost per Employee the union negotiating committee needs to specify the date (or period of time) it wants the data based on.

When the union requests information from the employer, including the number of employees on the seniority roster, their years of service, their wage classification and the like, that should identify the number of employees at that particular point in time in which the snapshot is taken. If employment levels have been particularly variable over a year or a large number of employees are in layoff status, or for some other reason are on the seniority list but are not working, the union committee may want to make some adjustment to the number of employees.

When a contractual benefit cost is expressed on the basis of Average Annual Cost per Employee a fixed number of employees must be based either on a certain date, on an average over the year, or on an adjusted number. This number should be used consistently across all the costing calculations.

Average Cost per Employee per Hour

The third way of expressing costs, Average Cost per Employee per Hour (Worked), is derived by dividing the Average Annual Cost per Employee by the number of hours worked per year.

The number of hours "worked" per year can be a point of particular discussion or controversy between the union and the employer. Do employees work 52 weeks per year or 52.2 weeks per year? Do they work forty hours a week or 48 hours, including overtime? What about the hours for which they are paid, but do not work (for instance, vacations and holidays)?

Most employers will say that they want to base an average hourly cost of contractual benefits on hours actually worked, or so-called 'productive hours'. It is likely obvious to the reader that the Average Cost per Employee per Hour for any particular contractual benefit will be larger if it is divided by a smaller number of 'hours worked'.

For instance, the value (cost) of eight paid holidays is $.77 per hour based on average straight-time wages of $25.00 per hour and 2,088 scheduled hours per year or $.85 per hour based on 1,888 productive (worked) hours per year. The difference is not really negligible but neither is it tragic if the union agrees to use productive hours in its calculations.

The reason to express benefits (costs) in this format is to be able to compare various contractual benefits in a simple, understandable way, usually by comparing a particular benefit to the average wage which is often expressed on an hourly basis.

Experienced union negotiators understand that the important consideration is to use the same figure for the number of hours in all costing calculations when expressing Average Cost per Employee per Hour. This ensures an 'apples with apples' comparison.

Throughout this manual 'Productive Hours' are defined as all scheduled and worked hours, including overtime hours, minus all paid hours not worked. Chapter 4 describes how such a calculation is made.

Requesting Data from the Employer

The union cannot begin to develop accurate cost estimates without requesting certain data from the employer. The employer is the repository for this information and the union has a clear legal right under the National Labor Relations Act (NLRA) to obtain necessary and relevant information from the employer for the purpose of collective bargaining. Obtaining information from the employer is the first step for the union negotiating committee to begin its preparations for bargaining.

Requesting data from the employer usually should be initiated between six and four months prior to the expiration of the contract. It is not recommended that the union send its information request in combination with its serving of notice to reopen and renegotiate its collective agreement. Since serving notice is normally done just a few days before the legally obligatory period (generally 60 days under the NLRA, but 90 days in the health care sector) requesting information at this point in time (and then waiting to receive it from the employer) does not permit the union negotiating committee sufficient opportunity to carefully analyze the information it has requested.

Requesting and receiving accurate and comprehensive data from the employer is one of the steps that will permit the union negotiating committee to have equal status at the negotiating table. But the union committee must take the time and put in the effort to format the data from the employer, to carefully examine it and undertake various tests to check its accuracy and reasonableness, and then develop its own analytical tools for using the data. Only then will the union committee be fully prepared to participate in the dynamics of negotiations without wondering if it is operating with one eye blind or whether the other side is 'telling the truth'.

The Employer's Duty to Provide Information[1]

Although the NLRA does not contain an explicit requirement that an employer provide the union with information, the National Labor Relations Board in some of its earliest decisions clearly stated that the intent of the law requires the parties to exchange information that is relevant to the bargaining process. In a 1936 case the Board wrote that "The interchange of ideas, communication of facts peculiarly within the knowledge of either party is the essence of the bargaining process." [Allen, S.L. and Co., Inc., 1 NLRB 714,728 (1936)].

The union, however, must generally first make a request for information and the request should be specific. Although a valid request for information can be made verbally, the union's initial request for information for negotiations should definitely be made in writing. As well, it makes sense to have some proof (for instance a Postal Service receipt or signature from an employer official) that the request was received by the employer. During the course of negotiations, verbal requests to clarify data or have data presented in a different way are certainly appropriate; this type of request should be clearly reflected in the union's bargaining notes or can be made in writing.

The information the union requests must have relevancy to the union's role as the employees' bargaining representative. The Board (supported by the courts) has found information on wages and related data to be presumptively relevant. Presumptively relevant means that the union is not required to justify to the employer why it is requesting this information – the courts have already decided that the union has a right to it. All of the types of information covered in this manual have been considered to be presumptively relevant.

An employer is not required to provide information in the precise form requested by the union. When an employer has an objection to the form in which the union

---

[1] Attorney Robert W. Sikkel published an excellent paper titled Duty to Furnish Information Under the National Labor Relations Act: A General Overview at the ABA Section of Labor and Employment Law, 2007 Annual CLE Conference:
//www.abanet.org/labor/annualconference/2007/materials/data/papers/v2/057.pdf

has requested information, it must advise the union of its objection and the employer is still obliged to cooperate with the union in finding an appropriate accommodation. The employer has an obligation to make a diligent effort to obtain information requested by the union but it is not required to gather or create information that it does not already possess. But all of the types of data discussed in this manual should be in the possession of an employer in one form or another.

An employer cannot object, per se, to the cost of assembling data for the union. The National Labor Relations Board has held under certain circumstances that an employer can ask the union to pay a reasonable cost to duplicate information that has been requested. But the general rule is that the parties should bargain over this issue and whether information has been supplied at no cost in the past has some precedence.

Finally, an employer cannot unreasonably delay producing information requested by the union. Whether a delay is unreasonable is determined based on the particular facts of the request. But for the types of data covered in this manual an employer should have no trouble assembling the information within a time-frame of several weeks. Obviously, the union negotiating committee or its chair should be in routine contact with his or her management counterpart after the information request has been sent to find out whether the employer has any questions, concerns or problems in assembling the information. A delay of more than one month should prompt the union to take swift action in the form of a clear statement to the employer that if information is not forthcoming in a week the union will file a charge with the National Labor Relations Board for violation of Section 8 (d).

The union should make the processing of its request for information as easy as possible for the employer and as easy as possible for itself in later using that information. There is no reason why the union should not request information in an electronic format if that makes it easier for the employer and easier for the union. Requesting data in an Excel or other spreadsheet format could make the employer's work easier and could save much duplicative data entry work for the union. In this manual the information received from the Regional Medical Center (RMC) is in an Excel worksheet. Though an employer may not transmit information exactly in the format shown in that worksheet, asking for certain information such as the number of workers in each classification, the wage rates, and a breakdown of seniority or vacation eligibility in electronic form can save the union a lot of effort and minimize errors.

Excel Basics – Opening workbooks and worksheets
An Excel file is called a 'workbook' rather than a document as in MS Word and the workbook itself consists of a set of 'worksheets' saved together under one file name. When Excel is opened, an empty workbook titled **Book 1** will appear. It is a series of columns beginning with **A** and continuing through the alphabet (and beyond) and a series of rows starting with **1** and continuing down the page. Book 1, by default, opens as three worksheets, labeled **Sheet 1** through **Sheet 3** which can be seen as tabs along the bottom edge of the Excel

window. Each worksheet can be given a name by double clicking on the tab and typing in the name; you can change the name by right-clicking the tab and choosing Rename from the menu. The entire workbook can be saved with a name of your choice with the normal Save As command.

After opening either the Format Workbook or the RMC Workbook, there is a series of ten worksheets, starting with 'Average Wage without Progression' and continuing to the last one named 'Data from the Employer'. To open a worksheet, just click on its tab. All worksheet tabs will not be visible. To scroll across and see the names of all worksheets, use the scroll button on the lower left corner of the page as shown in the following screen shot.

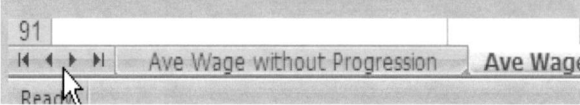

Chapter 2 – Wages and Salaries (without step progression)

CALCULATING AN AVERAGE straight-time (base) wage for the bargaining unit is the first critical piece of information that the union negotiating committee should prepare. This can be calculated on an hourly, weekly or monthly wage but it does not include overtime pay or other premiums.

The average straight-time wage rate is simply the average of every employee's wage in the bargaining unit. This average could be calculated by adding the wage rate/salary of each person in the bargaining unit and then dividing by that number of employees. For a bargaining unit of 20 employees this is quite easy to do but for larger units, it makes sense to use some standard mathematical formulas.

In most union contracts, there is a specific wage rate for each job classification or job title. Coupled with knowing how many employees are in each job classification or job title, multiplication will easily create subtotals for each job or wage classification. This is what is known as a 'weighted' average, because it is based on the number of employees working at each job classification, job title or job rate. Then summing these subtotals and dividing by the total number of employees will yield a 'weighted' average straight-time wage rate.

FORMAT WORKSHEET #1

Format Worksheet #1 shows a template for a spreadsheet that calculates the average straight-time wage for a bargaining unit in which there is no 'step progression' within a job classification/title – that is, everyone who holds that classification is paid at the contractual rate, perhaps with the exception of probationary employees who are discussed separately below.

In column A the names of the contractual job classifications will be typed in each row. In the sample format they are listed as classification A to classification Z. In column B the contractual wage rate for each classification is entered and in the title for that column the date at which the costing 'snapshot' is being taken should be entered.

Excel Basics – Modifying data in worksheets
There are several ways to modify or put your own information into Format Worksheet #1. When you click a cell and start typing, you will *automatically replace* the existing data. When you want to put your contract's actual job classifications or job titles in the sample format in column A, just click a cell (A4, A5, etc) and type; the alphabetical letters in the sample format will be replaced with your job classifications/titles.

You may want to keep some of the formatting in the worksheet such as column headings. If you only want to add an appropriate date, for instance, to the heading in cell B3, you can click on the cell but then do the *actual editing* in the **Formula Bar** at the top of the sheet. The advantage here is that you can delete just a portion of the text and add what you like. When the text is how you want it, hit Enter on the keyboard or click the Accept icon, which is the checkmark √.

Format Worksheet #1 - Average ST Hourly Wages (w/o Step Progression)

	A	B	C	D	E
1	Format Worksheet #1 - Average ST Hourly Wages (w/o Step Progression)				
2					
3	Classification	Wage Rate as of _____ (date)	Number of Employees	Classification Hourly SubTotal	Hourly Average
4	A			=B4*C4	
5	B			=B5*C5	
6	C			=B6*C6	
7	D			=B7*C7	
8	E			=B8*C8	
9	F			=B9*C9	
10	G			=B10*C10	
11	H			=B11*C11	
12	I			=B12*C12	
13	J			=B13*C13	
14	K			=B14*C14	
15	L			=B15*C15	
16	M			=B16*C16	
17	N			=B17*C17	
18	O			=B18*C18	
19	P			=B19*C19	
20	Q			=B20*C20	
21	R			=B21*C21	
22	S			=B22*C22	
23	T			=B23*C23	
24	U			=B24*C24	
25	V			=B25*C25	
26	W			=B26*C26	
27	X			=B27*C27	
28	Y			=B28*C28	
29	Z			=B29*C29	
30	TOTAL EEs and Total Hourly Wage		=SUM(C4:C29)	=SUM(D4:D29)	
31	Average Straight-Time Hourly (Base) Wage				=D30/C30

Column C will list the number of employees who hold each job classification. Column D is then used to calculate a subtotal of hourly wages for that particular classification. The formula for calculation of that subtotal in cell D4 is =B4*C4. The formula can be initially placed into Cell D4 by clicking cell D4; it will be 'highlighted' with a border; then in the Formula Bar you type the formula, always beginning with the = sign.

The basic operator symbols in Excel are + (plus sign) meaning addition; - (minus sign) meaning subtraction; * (asterisk) meaning multiplication; and / (slash) meaning division.

The formula is telling Excel to multiply the number in cell B4 (the wage rate) times the number in cell C4 (the number of employees) and to display the calculated result in cell D4.

The formula can also be entered without typing the actual cell locations. This is done by typing = in the cell in which you want the result of the formula (for example D4) to be displayed, then clicking on the first cell, B4, that you want included as part of the formula, entering the mathematical operator (+, -, * or /) and then clicking the remaining cell C4 and hitting Enter on the keyboard. When 'clicking' cells into formulas, Excel displays it in the Formula bar and also shows in 'living color' the cells that are being included in the formula.

Excel Basics – Formula essentials and Auto Sum

Excel always multiplies or divides before it adds or subtracts; if you want Excel to do otherwise you must bracket, with ( ) the numbers you want to be added or subtracted so that these operations are made first.

For example:
=C4+5*C5 means that C5 is multiplied by 5 and then C4 is added to the result.

=(C4+5)*C5 means that 5 is added to C4 and that result is multiplied by C5.

Cell C30 has the formula =SUM(C4:C29). This is one of the easiest Excel formulas to enter by using the Auto Sum function: the ∑ icon on the Excel toolbar. After clicking on cell C30 and it is highlighted (active), click the Auto Sum icon and Excel will highlight the cells that it *believes* should be added. If the 'flashing marquee' shows the correct cells to be added, in this case cells C4 through C29, then hit Enter and the formula has been created and the total number of employees will be summed and displayed in C30. Likewise, in cell D30 an Auto Sum of the classification subtotals has been entered.

The average hourly wage (the **weighted** average) is then the value in cell D30 (the sum of the classification subtotals) divided by the total number of employees in cell C30. The formula can be typed (or clicked into) cell E30 and is simply =D30/C30.

What if your contract has less (or more) than 27 job classifications/titles? To eliminate a row or a series of rows, highlight the row (or rows), then right-click and from the drop-down menu choose Delete. Adding a row is done by choosing Insert. Whenever rows are inserted or deleted Excel will adjust any formulas within the worksheet.

Data from the Regional Medical Center (RMC)

Worksheet #10 in both the Format Workbook and in the RMC Workbook has information that has been supplied by the employer to the union. Please have a look at that information. You may also want to print the two pages. Note that the Regional Medical Center essentially has only two job classifications. One classification, CM/CS Specialist, has three sub classifications: Bachelors, Bachelors+23 and Masters. There is also a classification for Part-time RNs which has two sub classifications: Associates and Bachelors.

There are 52 employees holding the classification of CM/CS Specialist and there are 44 part-time RNs. The total number of bargaining unit employees is 96 and the breakdown for each sub classification is shown in Worksheet #10.

Note that this particular contract has a 15-step wage progression for each of these five sub classifications. To make the most accurate estimate of the average straight-time (base) hourly wage it is necessary to know how many employees are in each sub classification and in each wage step. The calculation of the average wage with this 15-step progression will be described in Chapter 3.

But for now, for the sake of illustration, let's assume that this particular contract has no step progression. For this illustration we will use Step 8 to calculate an average wage. The Step 8 wage rate for CM/CS Specialist (Bachelors) is $17.9520; for CM/CS (Bachelors+23) it is $19.0081; and for CM/CS (Masters) it is $19.8924. For the part-time RNs (Associates) the wage rate is $14.5200 and for the part-time RNs (Bachelors) it is $16.8642.

Note that it is a little unusual for a collective agreement to have wage rates expressed to four decimal points (1/100 of a cent) but that is the case in this particular contract. Fortunately, when using Excel, the calculations can be easily made.

The wage rates have been entered in column B in the correct row and the number of employees in each sub classification is entered in column C in the correct rows.

The formula for calculating the Classification Hourly Subtotal in cell D5 is simply cell B5*C5. To actually 'complete' the formula the Enter key on the keyboard must be hit so that Excel knows that the entry into the cell is finished.

There are several ways in which this simple multiplication formula can be incorporated into the additional rows (i.e. for the other classifications). For example, you can click in cell D6 and again type or "click in" the formula (=B6*C6). But Excel has several easier ways.

Excel Basics – Copying and pasting cells
One method is to copy the formula in D5 and then paste it into other cells. For instance, you can click on cell D5, click copy (or use Ctrl+C or right click and choose copy from the shortcut menu) and the cell you are copying will be highlighted with a 'flashing marquee'. You then simply click on cell D6 and paste the formula there.

A cell that has been copied will remain 'active' and can be pasted over and over again until you 'de-activate' it by pressing Esc on your keyboard. But many times this feature is quite helpful as a copied cell containing a value or a formula can be pasted in multiple cell locations, for instance, down the whole of column D.

An easier way, albeit one to be used with some caution, is Excel's AutoFill command. This method permits the formula in one cell to be dragged (and copied) down a column of cells which have the same symmetrical format (i.e. the same formula will be used for cells in additional rows or columns).

AutoFill is accessed by clicking on the cell that contains the formula, in this case cell D5, and grabbing the 'fill handle' that resides at the lower right corner of the cell (see the position of the mouse pointer on the following screen shot of Worksheet #1a). When the mouse is positioned over this small black square, the pointer will turn into a small black cross (+). While holding down the left mouse button drag this + down through cell D6 to cell D7 and release the mouse. Excel will copy the formula from cell C5 to cells D6 and D7 (and automatically change the 'source' cells in the formula from row 5 to rows 6 and 7.

	A	B	C	D	E
1	RMC Worksheet #1a - Average ST Hourly Wages (w/o Step Progression)				
2					
3	Classification	Wage Rate as of 9/1/2008	Number of Employees	Classification Hourly SubTotal	
4	Full-time Employees				
5	Bachelors	17.952	34	=B5*C5	
6	Bachelors + 23	19.0081	11		
7	Masters	19.8924	7		
8	Part-time Employees				
9	Associates	14.52	34		
10	Bachelors	16.8642	10		
11	TOTAL EEs and Total Hourly Wages		=C5+C6+C7+C9+C10	=SUM(D5:D10)	
12	Average Straight-Time Hourly (Base) Wage			=D11/C11	

RMC Worksheet #1a shows the wage rates and number of employees that have been entered into the correct cells and the formula for the classification hourly subtotal for the first sub classification, which then needs to be copied to cells D6, D7, D9 and D10 using one of the methods described above.

The next step is to sum (add) the number of employees in column C and likewise sum the Classification Hourly Subtotals. To do this select Cell C11 and then enter a formula for adding Cells C5, C6, C7, C9 and C10. Cell C8 is not included because it is empty because of the subheading called Part-time employees.

To enter the sum, click in Cell C11, hit the = key and type C5+C6+C7+C9+C10 and then hit Enter. (Or each of the cells to be included in the sum can be 'clicked-in', putting a + sign before each additional cell). The formula will be shown in the formula bar as well as in cell C11, as shown above.

Excel provides a few other easier ways to put addition formulas into a worksheet. One way is to use the SUM mathematical operator (=SUM) and then enter the cells which are to be added, in this case D5 through D10 surrounded by parentheses and separated by a colon. The formula would read =SUM(D5:D10), as shown above. Note that this formula would add any value that is in the now-blank cell D8 so one must be careful when using this function.

As noted earlier, Auto Sum is an even easier way that usually works, **with some caution**. In this worksheet, if Auto Sum is attempted in cell D11, Excel will offer to sum just cells D10 and D9 because D8 is blank. Auto Sum works most reliably when there is a series of numbers to be added with no blank cells.

However, even in a series like this with a blank cell, Auto Sum can be used by clicking in cell D11, clicking Auto Sum, and then – while holding the left mouse key – dragging over the cells to be included as part of the sum. The formula, using this method would again be SUM(D5:D10). But remember, if a value is later entered into cell D8, it will be included as part of the sum; so be careful and always check your formulas. Lastly, cell E12 has the formula for calculating the average straight-time (base) wage: cell D11 divided by cell C11.

Excel Basics – Viewing worksheet formulas
There are several ways to check formulas while a worksheet is being constructed. When a cell that has a formula is clicked, the formula is seen in the Formula Bar. However, it can be time-consuming to click through many cells to check formulas. ALL the formulas plus the actual data that has been entered in the worksheet can be seen by holding down the Ctrl key and hitting the tilde key ~ (beneath the Esc key). This method will toggle back and forth between seeing the worksheet with formulas and the worksheet with the calculated values.

The screen shot of RMC Worksheet #1b, below, shows the data that have been entered into this simple worksheet and the calculated average straight-time hourly wage based on the formulas described above.

	A	B	C	D	E
1	RMC Worksheet #1b - Average ST Hourly Wages (w/o Step Progression)				
2					
3	Classification	Wage Rate as of 9/1/2008	Number of Employees	Classification Hourly SubTotal	
4	Full-time Employees				
5	Bachelors	$17.9520	34	$610.37	
6	Bachelors + 23	$19.0081	11	$209.09	
7	Masters	$19.8924	7	$139.25	
8	Part-time Employees				
9	Associates	$14.5200	34	$493.68	
10	Bachelors	$16.8642	10	$168.64	
11	TOTAL EEs and Total Hourly Wages		96	$1,621.03	
12	Average Straight-Time Hourly (Base) Wage				$16.89

The calculated Average Straight-Time (Base) Hourly Wage for this bargaining unit is $16.89 (rounded to the nearest cent) and this is a weighted average of the five sub classifications based on the number of employees in each sub classification.

But now the union committee might decide that it could be useful to also know the average wage for the full-time employees as a group and for the part-time employees as a group. There are several ways that this could be done but probably the easiest is to just insert two more rows into the worksheet which will provide additional cells in which these calculations can be made.

Excel Basics – Inserting new rows.

To insert a new row into a worksheet, click the row below where you want the insertion to be made. Do this by left clicking the row number on the far left of the worksheet; the entire row will be highlighted. Then right-click and a drop down menu will give you several options; you want to choose Insert. On Worksheet #1b, you would left-click on row 8, then right-click and choose Insert and replicate the same steps on row 11. There are now two additional rows.

These rows can be labeled as 'full-time subtotal' and 'part-time subtotal' and then formulas can be entered for calculating the average wage for each group. Note that Excel will keep previous formulas intact and will automatically change the cell designations in any formulas. Now Auto Sum is used to sum the number of part-time and full-time employees and their sub classification totals. To calculate the average wage for each group the wage totals are divided by the number of employees by clicking cell E8 then entering =D8/C8) and by clicking cell E12 and entering =D12/C12. The average wages for both groups are now calculated.

	A	B	C	D	E
1	RMC Worksheet #1c - Average ST Hourly Wages (w/o Step Progression)				
2					
3	Classification	Wage Rate as of 9/1/2008	Number of Employees	Classification Hourly SubTotal	
4	Full-time Employees				
5	Bachelors	$17.9520	34	$610.37	
6	Bachelors + 23	$19.0081	11	$209.09	
7	Masters	$19.8924	7	$139.25	
8		Full-time subtotal	52	$958.70	18.43661346
9	Part-time Employees				
10	Associates	$14.5200	34	$493.68	
11	Bachelors	$16.8642	10	$168.64	
12		Part-time subtotal	44	$662.32	15.05277273
13	TOTAL EEs and Total Hourly Wages		96	$1,621.03	
14	Average Straight-Time Hourly (Base) Wage				$16.89

However, the sum of the classification wage rates would now be incorrect because in column D an Auto Sum had been used and Excel would now add together each individual classification cell plus the two subtotal cells and calculate a totally nonsensical average wage for the entire bargaining unit.

Chapter 2 – Wages and Salaries (without step progression)

To avoid these mistakes, here are two pieces of advice: 1. Check formulas carefully; 2. Watch for nonsensical numbers after and while formulas are entered, particularly after new rows or new columns have been inserted. While Excel will usually make the needed adjustments to existing formulas to keep them correct, it will NOT automatically correct a formula like Auto Sum which captures all cells, including those from inserted rows or columns.

The incorrect formula in that cell must be removed. It is easy to do: click the cell and hit the Delete key. Then a correct formula can be entered, which in this case could be either a sum of the each of the five classifications: D13=D5+D6+D7+D10+D11 or more simply, just a sum of the two subtotals: D13=D8+D12. The screen shot of Worksheet #1c shows what the modified worksheet including the full-time and part-time employee subtotals would look like.

Note in RMC Worksheet #1 that the average wage for the full-time and part-time subtotals have 8 digits to the right of the decimal point – a level of significance that may be needed for nuclear physics but not for costing a collective agreement. Now some of the basic formatting tools in Excel will be reviewed, many of which are very similar to those available in Microsoft Word.

Excel Basics – Formatting Tools
Formatting a spreadsheet can sometimes seem daunting. An important thing to remember is that one can always undo formatting changes that are made in Excel just like they are undone in Microsoft Word by using the Undo icon in the toolbar. Indeed, in Excel Undo will work for multiple changes that have been made. And the Redo command can be used if what we have undone is incorrect.

Bold, italics and text
As in Word, cells can be made bold, italics, underlined as well as in different colors and highlighted. Making some headings bold also helps in readability. Keep in mind that Excel will always first treat data in a cell as a number rather than as text. If you keep your workbook cells in General Format, the default setting, cells can handle both text and numbers. But sometimes when you clearly want an explanatory label on a row or on a column, you can highlight the cell or group of cells (or entire row/column) and change the format to Text. The Excel toolbar provides this choice.

Number and currency format
Sometimes, you may want to clearly designate a cell, row or column in the general Number format or in the Currency format which will automatically insert a $ sign. In either the Currency or Number format the default value displayed is to two decimal points, for example 22.31. Even if you enter data such as 22.3096, the default display will be rounded to two decimal points unless you change the cell display format. This is simply done by selecting the cells and then clicking on the Increase Decimal icon on the toolbar. Likewise, you can use the Decrease Decimal icon when you require a less precise number.

Alignment
Excel will align text within a cell to the left and numbers to the right. But you have the option of changing that default (for instance to center data in certain cells) by

highlighting a cell, a group of cells, a row or a column and using the appropriate icon (left, center or right) on the toolbar.

Size and visibility
Worksheets can become huge with too many columns and rows for the information to be readable and user-friendly. There are many ways to 'skin the cat' in presenting and printing your worksheets. For instance, you can select only part of a sheet and designate it as the print area or you can temporarily hide designated columns and rows that are not absolutely necessary for someone else to see.

But with some advance thinking and by using some of Excel's formatting tools you can make your worksheets look as understandable as possible. All of the worksheets in the Format Workbook have been designed so that they will print portrait style on standard letter-sized paper.

Wrap Text
Two important tools for you to master are Wrap Text and Merge & Center. Wrap Text allows you to have a fairly long text title for a column even if the rest of the column has only two-digit numbers. For example, in Worksheet #1, the heading 'Number of Employees' spread across a column is not necessary when it can be 'wrapped' within a narrower column using Wrap Text. Try for clarity in meaning for every column heading while still keeping them as short as possible. But keep in mind that too many abbreviations or code words will make it difficult for someone else to understand the basis of your worksheet. You can also use Text Wrap for row headings but doing so often makes it more difficult to understand as rows will not be of equivalent size on the worksheet. Try to keep row titles as short as possible and keep them on one line.

Merge & Center
Merge & Center is most useful for titles and for the summarizing rows in your worksheet in which there is no data in a cell or cells to the right of your text. If you look at Format Worksheet #1 you will notice that the title covers all five columns from A to E. You do this by typing the title in cell A1 – you will see it all displayed in the formula bar and, as long as there is no other data in cells B1, C1, D1 and E1, you will see it across all the columns after you have hit the Enter key. By highlighting cells A1 to E1 and then clicking Merge and Center you 'spread' the title across all five columns. If you want the text merged but not centered, you can merge the cells and then left justify the text

Deleting rows
Earlier we reviewed how a row can be added to a worksheet. What if we have an extra, unnecessary row? To eliminate the entire row, you left-click on the row number and it will be highlighted, then right-click and choose Delete from the drop-down menu. Note that if you just use the Delete key on the keyboard, you will clear the data in the row, but the row itself will still be there, albeit with empty values all the way across. You can also choose Clear from the drop-down menu which will do the same as the Delete key.

Inserting and deleting columns
Columns can be inserted and deleted following similar steps. Highlight a column by left-clicking on its column letter, then right click and choose Insert. The new column will be inserted to the left of the

column you highlighted. You can also clear the contents of all cells in a column, rather than deleting the column itself.

Adjusting column width
Excel will automatically adjust column width if you want it to do so but doing it 'by hand' is simple and functional. Just place your cursor on the line between two columns (at the top of the page), hold the left mouse key and narrow or widen the column. You will easily be aware if certain numbers are not being displayed because your column is too narrow. The cell will show ######### all across it. You can adjust the width as described above or place your cursor at the right edge of the column and it will turn to a double-headed arrow, then double-click and the column will automatically adjusted to the 'Best Fit'.

What about Probationary Employees?

Many union contracts provide for a probationary wage rate prior to advancing to a classification or job wage rate. Probationary employees must be included in the calculation of the average straight-time wage rate. If a significant number of employees are working at a probationary rate because of a large number of new hires, probationary rates should be added to the spreadsheet. For each job classification in which employees are working at a probationary wage rate an additional row would be added with the applicable wage rate and the number of employees. If there is a small number of probationary employees or the length of the probationary period is short, these employees can be included with employees at the non-probationary classification rate. It will have the effect of slightly overstating the employer's actual wage cost.

It is important that all employees in the bargaining unit be included in the calculation of the average straight-time wage rate.

Chapter 3 – Wages and Salaries (with step progression)

A SLIGHTLY MORE difficult challenge comes from contracts that have 'step progression' within wage classifications, especially if there are many steps and the progression occurs over a long period of time (for example, 5 or more years). For these situations the spreadsheet needs to be expanded to permit calculation of an average classification rate based on the number of employees in each progression step.

FORMAT WORKSHEET #2

The layout for Format Worksheet #2 is very similar to #1 except that Column B now has significance and has the Step Wage Rate for each of the contractual classifications. In this sample format four classifications (A to D) and six step rates for each classification are shown, from the Start Rate through to the Top Rate for each classification. The format can be easily modified by inserting additional rows or 'blocks' of rows. If a contract has a uniform number of step progressions for each job classification then it is easiest to develop the format for the first classification, including the calculation formulas, and then copy and paste that entire 'block' for each successive job classification. Simply highlight the block of cells you want to copy, use the copy function, click in the **one cell** where you want the 'copy' to start again and paste.

The formulas in Worksheet #2, shown below, are straightforward. Each step rate is multiplied by the number of employees in that step and the subtotal is displayed in Column E. A formula for calculating the Total Number of Employees in each classification (cells D10, D18, etc.) and a sum of Total Hourly Wages for all steps within each classification is made (cells E10, E18, etc.). An average rate for each classification is calculated by dividing E10 by D10, E18 by D18, and so forth. Those average rates are shown in cells E11, E19, E27 and E35.

Finally, to determine an Average Straight-Time Hourly Wage for the entire bargaining unit, the total number of employees in each classification and the Total Hourly Wages for each classification must be summed. In Worksheet #2, these are shown in cells D44 and E44 and the overall average wage for the bargaining unit is displayed in cell E45.

	A	B	C	D	E
1	Format Worksheet #2 - Average ST Hourly Rate (with Step Progression)				
2					
3	Classification		Wage Rate as of (date)	Number of Employees	Classification Hourly SubTotal
4	A	Start Rate			=C4*D4
5	A	Step 1			=C5*D5
6	A	Step 2			=C6*D6
7	A	Step 3			=C7*D7
8	A	Step 4			=C8*D8
9	A	Top Rate			=C9*D9
10	TOTAL # of EEs and Total Hourly Wages for A			=SUM(D4:D9)	=SUM(E4:E9)
11	Average Rate for Classification A				=E10/D10
12	B	Start Rate			=C12*D12
13	B	Step 1			=C13*D13
14	B	Step 2			=C14*D14
15	B	Step 3			=C15*D15
16	B	Step 4			=C16*D16
17	B	Top Rate			=C17*D17
18	TOTAL # of EEs and Total Hourly Wages for B			=SUM(D12:D17)	=SUM(E12:E17)
19	Average Rate for Classification B				=E18/D18
20	C	Start Rate			=C20*D20
21	C	Step 1			=C21*D21
22	C	Step 2			=C22*D22
23	C	Step 3			=C23*D23
24	C	Step 4			=C24*D24
25	C	Top Rate			=C25*D25
26	TOTAL # of EEs and Total Hourly Wages for C			=SUM(D20:D25)	=SUM(E20:E25)
27	Average Rate for Classifcation C				=E26/D26
28	D	Start Rate			=C28*D28
29	D	Step 1			=C29*D29
30	D	Step 2			=C30*D30
31	D	Step 3			=C31*D31
32	D	Step 4			=C32*D32
33	D	Top Rate			=C33*D33
34	TOTAL # of EEs and Total Hourly Wages for D			=SUM(D28:D33)	=SUM(E28:E33)
35	Average Rate for Classifcation D				=E34/D34
36	E				
37	F				
38	G				
39	H				
40	I				
41	J				
42	K				
43	L				
44	TOTAL # of Employees and Total Hourly Wages			=D10+D18+D26+D34	=E10+E18+E26+E34
45	Average Straight-Time Hourly Wage				=E44/D44

Data from the Regional Medical Center

Wage data from the Regional Medical Center has been added to RMC Worksheet #2 for the three full-time and two part-time classifications and each classification's 15 Step Rates as of September 1, 2008. Additionally, the number of employees in each step of the wage scale is entered. The step wage rates are taken from Worksheet

#10 – the information supplied by the Regional Medical Center.

It is worth noting here that each of the individual step wage rates can be typed into the worksheet but if a contract has an equal increment between each step it is much easier to enter the data by using a formula. In the case of the Regional Medical Center the increment increase between each step in the progression is exactly 1.8 percent. If your contract is of such a type, save some time and effort and prepare a formula. This could also be useful in the event that the negotiating committee wishes to examine the value of increasing (or decreasing) the incremental spread between steps. The screenshot below shows the data for the first job classification (CM/CS Bachelors) with its step wage rates and the number of employees, as well as the total number of employees in the classification and their Average Hourly Rate.

	A	B	C	D	E
1	RMC Worksheet #2 - Average ST Hourly Rate (with Step Progression)				
2					
3	Classification	Step	Wage Rate as of 9/1/08	Number of Employees	Classification Hourly SubTotal
4	CM/CS Bachelors	0	$15.5643	2	$31.13
5	CM/CS Bachelors	1	$15.8445	1	$15.84
6	CM/CS Bachelors	2	$16.1297	2	$32.26
7	CM/CS Bachelors	3	$16.4200	0	$0.00
8	CM/CS Bachelors	4	$16.7156	3	$50.15
9	CM/CS Bachelors	5	$17.0164	2	$34.03
10	CM/CS Bachelors	6	$17.3227	3	$51.97
11	CM/CS Bachelors	7	$17.6345	0	$0.00
12	CM/CS Bachelors	8	$17.9520	5	$89.76
13	CM/CS Bachelors	9	$18.2751	0	$0.00
14	CM/CS Bachelors	10	$18.6040	4	$74.42
15	CM/CS Bachelors	11	$18.9389	2	$37.88
16	CM/CS Bachelors	12	$19.2798	0	$0.00
17	CM/CS Bachelors	13	$19.6269	0	$0.00
18	CM/CS Bachelors	14	$19.9801	4	$79.92
19	CM/CS Bachelors	15	$20.3398	6	$122.04
20	TOTAL EEs and Total Hourly Wages forCM/CS Bachelors			34	$619.39
21	Average Hourly Rate for forCM/CS Bachelors				$18.22

The following screen shot shows the same part of the worksheet, and slightly more, with the formulas revealed. Note that the wage rate for CM/CS Bachelors Step 1 in cell C5 is based on the formula C4*1.018. To construct this series of wage rates it is necessary to enter the starting step, $15.5643, in C4 and then the formula in C5.

It is not necessary to reenter the formula for subsequent cells. For a shortcut use Excel's click and drag Auto Fill function to complete the formulas for each wage progression step from Step 2 to Step 15. To do this, grab the *fill handle* at the lower right corner of cell C5 by holding down the left mouse, dragging down to cell C19 and releasing the mouse. Excel will copy the formula, appropriately adjusted, to cells C6 through C19.

	A	B	C	D	E
1	RMC Worksheet #2 - Average ST Hourly Rate (with Step Progression)				
2					
3	Classification	Step	Wage Rate as of 9/1/08	Number of Employees	Classification Hourly SubTotal
4	CM/CS Bachelors	0	15.5643	2	=C4*D4
5	CM/CS Bachelors	1	=C4*1.018	1	=C5*D5
6	CM/CS Bachelors	2	=C5*1.018	2	=C6*D6
7	CM/CS Bachelors	3	=C6*1.018	0	=C7*D7
8	CM/CS Bachelors	4	=C7*1.018	3	=C8*D8
9	CM/CS Bachelors	5	=C8*1.018	2	=C9*D9
10	CM/CS Bachelors	6	=C9*1.018	3	=C10*D10
11	CM/CS Bachelors	7	=C10*1.018	0	=C11*D11
12	CM/CS Bachelors	8	=C11*1.018	5	=C12*D12
13	CM/CS Bachelors	9	=C12*1.018	0	=C13*D13
14	CM/CS Bachelors	10	=C13*1.018	4	=C14*D14
15	CM/CS Bachelors	11	=C14*1.018	2	=C15*D15
16	CM/CS Bachelors	12	=C15*1.018	0	=C16*D16
17	CM/CS Bachelors	13	=C16*1.018	0	=C17*D17
18	CM/CS Bachelors	14	=C17*1.018	4	=C18*D18
19	CM/CS Bachelors	15	=C18*1.018	6	=C19*D19
20	TOTAL EEs and Total Hourly Wages for CM/CS Bachelors			=SUM(D4:D19)	=SUM(E4:E19)
21	Average Hourly Rate for CM/CS Bachelors				=E20/D20
22	CM/CS Bachelors+23	0	16.48	0	=C22*D22
23	CM/CS Bachelors+23	1	=C22*1.018	1	=C23*D23
24	CM/CS Bachelors+23	2	=C23*1.018	0	=C24*D24

After the basic format for calculating average wages for each classification (using either Worksheet #1 or #2) is set up, then other useful calculations can be added to the worksheet. For instance, for the Regional Medical Center contract it may be helpful to know the average wage for all of the full-time employees and the average wage for the part-time employees. In other contracts one may wish to select and aggregate job classifications in particular departments or particular facilities if the collective agreement covers multiple sites.

The screen shot below captures formulas from the bottom part of the RMC worksheet in which the overall average straight-time hourly wage is calculated as well as the average rate for the full-time (F-T) and the part-time (P-T) classifications. Three additional calculations are included on this worksheet: the Total Annual Straight-Time Payroll for the RMC as well as the annual payroll for full-time and part-time employees. Note that these totals are based on the average straight-time hourly wage times the number of productive hours. The concept of productive hours is

Chapter 3 – Wages and Salaries (with step progression)

explained in the following chapter.

	A	B	C	D	E
92	TOTAL # of EEs and Total Hourly Wages for P-T RN Ba			=SUM(D76:D91)	=SUM(E76:E91)
93	Average Rate for P-T RN Bachelors				=E92/D92
94					
95	TOTAL # of Employees and Total Hourly Wages			=D92+D74+D56+D38+D20	=E92+E74+E56+E38+E20
96	Average Straight-Time Hourly Wage as of 9/1/08:				=E95/D95
97					
98	Average ST Hourly Rate for F-T CM/CS Classification:				=(E20+E38+E56)/FTEmp
99	Average ST Hourly Rate for P-T RN Classification:				=(E92+E74)/PTEmp
100					
101	Annual Payroll for F-T CM/CS Classification:				=E98*'Productive Hours'!E4
102	Annual Payroll for P-T RN Classification:				=E99*'Productive Hours'!E5
103	TOTAL Annual ST Payroll based on Scheduled Hours				=SUM(E101:E102)

A Few More Points on Calculating Average Straight-Time Wages

As noted earlier in this manual, this calculation should be considered as an accurate estimate of the average straight-time (base) hourly wage for the bargaining unit **at a particular point in time.** The workplace is not static and employees may be moving from one classification to another and some will be moving to their next step increase on their seniority date (or some other time period). Some higher paid employees may retire and be replaced by employees at lower rates. New employees might start at a probationary rate. Entirely new job classifications might be negotiated during the term of a contract. It is not entirely possible to predict the overall impact of these types of movements. They can, however, be captured in a subsequent snapshot taken at the end of a contract year or when preparing for the next round of negotiations.

In Chapter 11 a method for estimating the impact of what is sometimes called 'seniority creep' or 'longevity drift' is covered to account for employees moving into a higher wage step as well as employees advancing to a greater number of weeks of vacation eligibility.

There are several additional caveats concerning part-time employees, "red circled" employees and 'per-diem' employees or other employees without a fixed employment relationship who still may be covered under the terms of the collective agreement.

Unless there is a significant number of 'red-circled' employees who are being paid at a rate higher than their current classification or step wage rate or the union has a particular desire to examine the additional cost/benefit of the 'red-circled' employees' additional earnings, then these employees can be slotted into their appropriate position in the job classifications/step scales. Obviously, the employer's actual cost will be higher, but this will be negligible unless a considerable proportion of the bargaining unit is 'red-circled'.

The average *hourly* wage of part-time employees can be calculated using a format like either Worksheet #1 or #2 as was done for the part-time classifications in the Regional Medical Center contract. The overall impact on the total cost to the employer due to their reduced hours of work will be captured when their number of hours worked are applied to their average wage.

In bargaining units with a significant number of part-time employees, the union may want to construct a separate spreadsheet with data on the number of part-time employees, their hours of work and their wage/step classifications.

Because part-time employees often do not receive the same benefits as full-time employees (e.g. less vacation, fewer holidays or different insurance coverage), it is important for the union to know the number of part-time employees and which benefits to which they are entitled.

The issue of per diem employees or other contingent employees who may or may not be in the bargaining unit is different. Per diem employees often have a different wage scale, may have different premiums based on shifts worked, years of experience or number of hours actually worked in a pay period. Data on per diem employees should be requested from the employer and the union should prepare additional analytical spreadsheets for those employees. It is also important to carefully review the types of premium payments (e.g. shift, weekend, holiday premiums) to which per diem employees may be entitled.

Chapter 4 – Productive Hours

THE CONCEPT OF PRODUCTIVE hours is used to express the cost of contractual benefits over a common base – the average number of hours worked by members of the bargaining unit.

The union and employer may also agree for the purposes of convenience and simplicity to use another reasonable number of hours per year (e.g. 2,000) as the common base upon which to express the costs of wage-related premiums and other non-wage related contractual benefits on an hourly basis.

FORMAT WORKSHEET #3

Worksheet #3 lays out the fundamental methodology for calculating Productive Hours.

It is appropriate to request from the employer the actual number of hours worked, both straight-time and overtime hours, and the number of hours paid but not worked for contractual benefits such as holidays, vacation, sick leave, union business and the myriad of other similar un-worked but paid time. Even when the employer provides this information, the union should still make a few simple calculations to double check the reasonableness of the hours reported by the employer. Remember that even if an hour of overtime is paid at a premium rate it is still just one hour worked.

As shown below, Total Hours worked (scheduled) can be calculated by multiplying the number of full-time employees times their regular weekly hours (i.e. those that are not paid at a premium rate) times the weeks worked in a year (usually expressed as 52.2 weeks in a year). The same method is applied for part-time employees and, if needed, additional rows could be inserted for other contingent or "per diem" employees.

To the total scheduled hours, the number of overtime hours worked is added. The union must request this information from the employer, and as discussed in the next chapter, it is helpful to have a breakdown of the types of overtime hours: over 40 hours in a week, over 8 hours in a day, call-in hours, etc. depending upon the types of premium payments for time worked provided in the collective agreement.

From the total number of hours worked, hours that were paid but not worked are subtracted. In Format Worksheet #3, categories are listed for Vacations, Holidays, Sick Leave (it should reflect only sick leave hours actually taken, not the total that might be "banked") and Other. Additional rows with descriptive headings can be added to the worksheet if it is desired to capture other paid time-off information separately. The paid hours not worked are summed and then subtracted from the total hours worked. The format also shows a calculation for the Average Productive Hours per Employee. It is helpful to make this calculation just as a quick double check that the total Productive Hours per Year is reasonable. Note that the formula in Cell E15 is =E13/TotEmp.

Excel Basics – Naming cells
A cell or a range of cells in a worksheet can be given a meaningful name in addition to its column and row position. Often, this is quite helpful for certain pieces of data that are expected to be used in multiple places throughout a workbook. A name for a cell can be set to apply to just one worksheet or to the entire workbook. There are some rules about how you can name your cells and Excel's Help function describes the letter combinations that *cannot* be used. In the Format Workbook and the RMC Workbook, Cell G26 in Worksheet #10, Data from Employer, the total number of employees was named TotEmp. The value of naming a cell is that in any additional formulas that are constructed the cell name TotEmp can be used rather than the actual cell location. Cells are given names in the box to the left of the Formula Bar.

	A	B	C	D	E
1	Format Worksheet #3 - Calculation of Productive Hours				
2					
3		# of Employees	Regular Weekly Hours	Weeks per Year	TOTAL HOURS
4	F-T EEs' regular scheduled hours				=B4*C4*D4
5	P-T EEs' regular scheduled hours				=B5*C5*D5
6	+ Overtime hours worked				
7	TOTAL Hours Worked				=SUM(E4:E6)
8	- Paid vacation hours				
9	- Paid holiday hours				
10	- Paid sick hours				
11	- Other paid leave hours				
12	TOTAL Paid Hours Not Worked				=SUM(E8:E11)
13	Productive Hours Per Year				=E7-E12
14					
15	Average Productive Hours Per Employee				=E13/TotEmp
16					

Data from the Regional Medical Center

The only specific piece of data provided by the Regional Medical Center on hours worked was that 5,490 hours were worked at a premium of 1.5 times the hourly wage rate. No data was provided on vacation hours, holiday hours, sick leave or other hours paid but not worked. However, the contract specifies that employees are entitled to 10 paid holidays in a year; the contract has the vacation eligibility schedule and the union knows the years of service of employees from the seniority list.

The contract specifies that full-time employees are entitled to 3 paid personal days each year and part-time employees get two such days. The Regional Medical Center provided the union with information about the Total Annual Cost for sick leave and for bereavement leave. From this information, and a little bit of elbow grease, an estimate can be made of the previous year's Total Paid Hours Not Worked.

These 'reverse calculations' of hours paid but not worked are made in Worksheet #5, Pay for Non-Work Time so moving sequentially down the series of worksheets, the calculation of Productive Hours cannot yet be completed.

But this opportunity can be used to illustrate another important aspect of building Excel worksheets that are linked together in a single workbook. Cells in one worksheet can be 'referenced' to a cell in another worksheet, either by cell column and row location or by name. However, when working across worksheets Excel must be told on which worksheet the appropriate cell is located. Note on the screen shot below that in cells B4 and B5, the reference is only to 'named' cells FTEmp (the number of full-time employees) and PTEmp (the number of part-time employees). These were named, as TotEmp was, in Worksheet #10, Data from Employer.

The calculation of Total Hours scheduled by the employees is a simple formula in cells E4 and E5. The total overtime hours worked are added with a simple sum formula. From this sum, the paid hours not worked are subtracted. The referenced cells for these hours in cells E8–E11 are explained below.

	A	B	C	D	E
1	RMC Worksheet #3 - Calculation of Productive Hours				
2					
3		# of Employees	Regular Weekly Hours	Weeks per Year	TOTAL HOURS
4	F-T regular scheduled hours	=FTEmp	40	52.2	=B4*C4*D4
5	P-T regular scheduled hours	=PTEmp	30	52.2	=B5*C5*D5
6	+ Overtime hours worked				5490
7	TOTAL Scheduled Hours + OT hours				=SUM(E4:E6)
8	- Paid vacation hours				=Vacations!C9
9	- Paid holiday hours				='Pay for Non-Work Time'!B6
10	- Paid sick hours				='Pay for Non-Work Time'!B19
11	- Other paid leave hours				='Pay for Non-Work Time'!B14+'Pay for Non-Work Time'!B25
12	TOTAL Paid Hours Not Worked				=SUM(E8:E11)
13	Productive Hours Per Year				=E7-E12
14					
15	Average Productive Hours Per Employee				=E13/TotEmp

Excel Basics - Moving between worksheets
It may seem a little bit daunting at first to move between worksheets but with a little bit of practice and after giving your worksheets meaningful names, it becomes quite easy. An Excel workbook opens by default with three worksheets named Sheet 1, Sheet 2 and Sheet 3 but you can add your own descriptive name to a worksheet by right clicking the worksheet tab at the bottom of the Excel page and typing the name.

How many tabs you actually can see at one time depends upon how long the names are and the size of your screen. You can also adjust the screen view by placing your mouse pointer on the "tab split bar" (see below at pointer) and when it becomes a double-headed arrow, dragging it to the left or right to view fewer or more sheet tabs.

But you can easily scroll forward across all the worksheets in your workbook and scroll back: using the first arrow button on the far left will move you to the first sheet tab, the fourth arrow button will move you to the last sheet or the two center arrows move you forward or backward one sheet tab at a time until you can see the tab that you want. Click on the tab and that worksheet will open.

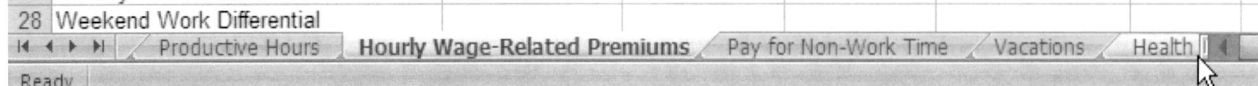

The calculations required to complete the Productive Hours worksheet are drawn from other worksheets and are referenced in the appropriate cell. The number of vacation hours paid but not worked is referenced to the worksheet named Vacations, and specifically from cell C9. The number of paid holiday hours is taken from the Pay for Non-Work Time worksheet, specifically cell B6. And note that other paid leave hours is the sum of cells B14 and B25 in the Pay for Non-Work Time worksheet.

When referencing a cell from another worksheet the name of that worksheet must be preceded with a single quotation mark (') and ended with an identical mark and the cell reference is preceded with an exclamation mark (!). All this can be typed into Excel's formula bar but it is much easier to just "click" in the cell reference formula. The method is described below.

Finally, the TOTAL Paid Hours Not Worked is calculated by summing cells E8:E11 and Productive Hours per Year are the total hours worked (E7) less the paid hours not worked (E12). The Average Productive Hours per Employee is calculated in cell E15. It was named PHrs in the RMC workbooks and will be referenced throughout the rest of the manual when calculating the average hourly cost of contractual benefits.

Excel Basics – Referencing cells across worksheets

Now that the movement between worksheets is clear, the steps for linking a formula in a cell in one worksheet to a cell in another using just a mouse click can be described. Here is how it goes: click in the cell in which you want to enter the 'linked reference cell; type = and then move to the worksheet from which you want to create the link; click that cell; hit Enter on your keyboard and voila! the cell is referenced. As noted earlier, you can even click on multiple cells in the linked worksheet by entering an appropriate operand (+, -, *, /) between clicks. This is how cell E11 of RMC Worksheet #3, above, was referenced to the sum of cells B14 and B25 from the Pay for Non-Work Time worksheet.

Chapter 5 – Hourly Wage-Related Premium Payments

EVERY UNION CONTRACT includes premium payments for certain types of work performed. The most common, of course, is a premium for work over the normal scheduled hours – overtime premiums. Overtime premiums can be paid for work in excess of 40 hours in a week, work in excess of 8 hours in a day or there can be additional premiums for other levels of hours per day or week.

It is also common to find shift differentials, weekend work differentials, and premiums for early call-in or after shift call-back in addition to overtime premiums. As well, some contracts specify premium pay for specific skills, certifications or specific responsibilities. The variety of premiums is quite broad; the key concept in this chapter for costing these kinds of benefits is that they are **based on hours actually worked**.

FORMAT WORKSHEET #4

Format Worksheet #4 has a format for calculating the costs/benefits associated with these types of wage-related premium payments. The distinguishing feature of these premiums/differentials is that they are paid on an hourly basis (in either a flat amount or a percentage amount) for hours actually worked. If a premium is not paid hourly or based on hours worked (for instance, an annually-paid premium such as a 'yearly weekend bonus', or a penalty payment such as 'paid sleep day' or a fixed 'on-call' bonus) they can be classified as either pay for time not worked (Worksheet #5) or as an annual payment and allowance (Worksheet #8).

Overtime Premiums

There are several possible approaches a union bargaining committee can take in assembling data on overtime premiums. The easiest way is to ask the employer to provide the aggregate Total Annual Cost for overtime premiums for the past year (or the past two or three years). But the union negotiating committee may want to have more detail for its decision-making about the types of overtime payments included in this aggregate amount and at what levels. The committee may also want to double check the accuracy of the information provided from the employer and that will be difficult, if not impossible, if the union only obtains an aggregate dollar amount for overtime premiums. Some employers might include the pay for the straight-time hour as well as the actual premium. For costing purposes, the premium alone needs to be captured.

For these reasons it makes sense to request information on overtime hours worked AND total overtime payments for each distinct type of overtime premium in the contract. The top part of Format Worksheet #4 shown below provides a basic method to calculate the Total OT Cost based on data for the number of overtime hours worked for various kinds of premiums. This format lists only premiums of 1 ½ times the hourly wage for weekly hours > 40; a daily premium of 1 ½ times for work > 8 hours and double-time for daily hours > x hours. Additional types of overtime premiums can be inserted into the format by adding an additional row(s) after row 6.

	A	B	C	D	E
1	**Format Worksheet #4 - Hourly Wage-Related Premium Payments**				
2					
3	Type of Overtime Premium	Amount of Hourly Premium	# of OT Hours Paid	Average S-T Base Wage	TOTAL OT COST
4	1 1/2 for Weekly > 40 hours	0.5		=AveST	=B4*C4*D4
5	1 1/2 Daily > 8 hours	0.5		=AveST	=B5*C5*D5
6	2 X Daily > x hours	1		=AveST	=B6*C6*D6
7	ANNUAL COST				=SUM(E4:E6)
8	ANNUAL COST PER EMPLOYEE				=E7/TotEmp
9	AVERAGE COST PER HOUR				=E8/PHrs
10					

It is important to remember that in this worksheet the *premium cost* for overtime is being calculated. If employees are paid 1 1/2 times their regular base rate for all hours over 40 in a workweek, the *actual premium is 1/2 (0.5) of their regular rate* for those hours worked in excess of 40. The employees also received pay at their regular rate for the overtime hours actually worked. Here only the premium portion is being captured. Likewise, if an employee receives double-time for certain hours, the premium is 1.0 times the hours worked times the regular base rate.

In this worksheet the # of OT Hours Paid is multiplied by the Average Straight-Time (Base) Wage that was previously calculated in Worksheet #1 or #2. This assumes that overtime premiums are spread equally across the bargaining unit. However, if only a few highly paid or lower paid classifications perform most of the overtime work, the union may want to use a different figure. By requesting the total overtime cost from the employer as well as the number of overtime hours worked, the union can easily make a 'reverse calculation' and determine the average wage of those who worked that overtime.

Note that in cells D4, D5 and D6 the actual figure for the average straight-time base wage could be entered. But it makes much more sense to link these cells to the calculation of average wage made in either Worksheet #1 or #2. That way, making adjustments or projections to the average wage in those worksheets will automatically be reflected in the costs/benefits of the overtime premiums. This named cell, AveST, which is either cell E31 from Format Worksheet #1 or cell E45 from Format Worksheet #2, can now be used in any other place or in any formula in the workbook when the Average Straight-Time Hourly Wage is to be used in a calculation.

One final comment on the summary portion of the worksheet: the ANNUAL COST is the sum of all the overtime premiums and the AVERAGE COST PER EMPLOYEE is calculated in cell E8 by dividing E7 by TotEmp (the total number of employees) and finally in cell E9, the AVERAGE COST PER HOUR is calculated by dividing by PHrs – the number of productive hours calculated in Worksheet #3.

Data from the Regional Medical Center

In the RMC collective agreement the only overtime premium is 1½ time base pay for weekly hours exceeding 40. The information provided to the union is that 5,490 overtime hours were worked. The screen shot below of RMC Worksheet #4 shows the ANNUAL COST, the ANNUAL COST PER EMPLOYEE and the AVERAGE COST PER HOUR for the RMC, based on the average straight-time hourly wage calculated in Worksheet #2.

	A	B	C	D	E
1	RMC Worksheet #4 - Hourly Wage-Related Premium Payments				
2					
3	Type of Overtime Premium	Amount of Hourly Premium	# of OT Hours Paid	Average S-T Base Wage	TOTAL OT COST
4	1 1/2 for Weekly > 40 hours	0.5	5,490	$ 17.07	$46,853.94
5	1 1/2 Daily > 8 hours				
6	2 X Daily > x hours				
7	ANNUAL COST				$46,853.94
8	ANNUAL COST PER EMPLOYEE				$488.06
9	AVERAGE COST PER HOUR				$0.29
10					

Shift Differentials

Union contracts often provide hourly differentials for shift work, usually expressed as 2nd shift (afternoon or evening) and 3rd shift (night or graveyard). Shift differentials are paid as an additional amount for hours worked during that shift (for instance, $3.25 per hour worked on night shift) or as a percent of an employee's wage rate (e.g. 12% shift differential for hours worked on night shift). Some union contracts also specify that employees are paid for eight hours for 7 1/2 or 7 hours work. This last type of premium will not be considered in this manual.

The union negotiating committee should request data from the employer on its annual costs for shift differentials. Again, the information will be better if it provides a breakdown of the annual cost of shift differential for each shift, the number of employees regularly assigned to each shift and the average number of hours they worked. This allows the union to check the validity of the information provided by the employer.

The cost of shift differentials based on a flat dollar and cents amount are quite easy to calculate. Multiply the differential amount times the number of employees working on that shift times the annual hours they work on that shift. In real life it may not be quite as straightforward in that the number of employees assigned to shifts with differentials might change over the course of the year and the number of hours actually worked 'on-shift' may be different from the average. And employees who normally work on the day shift may temporarily replace employees on a premium shift during vacations, sick leave or other circumstances. The recommendation is to request a figure from the employer for TOTAL ANNUAL COST for various shift differentials and double check its reasonableness by making some calculations as in Worksheet #4.

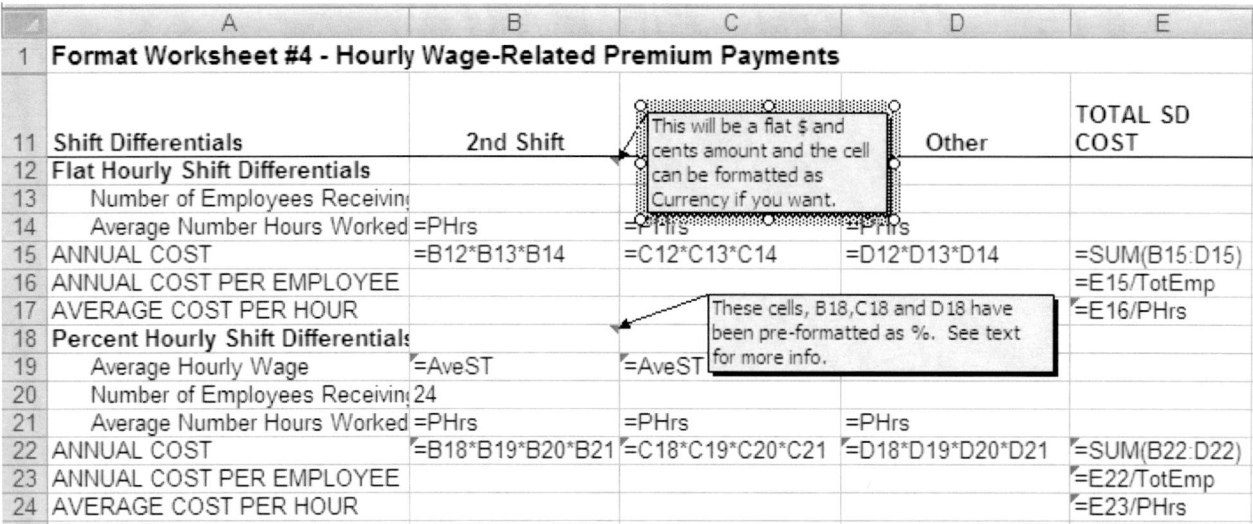

The shift differentials portion of Format Worksheet #4 is divided into a part for flat hourly shift differentials and a part for percent hourly shift differentials with 2nd and 3rd shift noted in columns B and C and column D available for another type of shift differential, perhaps rotating shifts.

Excel Basics – Comments in cells
Note the comments that are inserted into cells B12 and B18. These are marked with a red triangle in the upper-right of the cell and are made visible by rolling your cursor over the triangle or telling Excel to show all comments. The first comment is straight-forward: enter the amount of the flat shift differential in dollar and/or cents (e.g., 1.85 or .93) and if you format the cells as 'Currency' from the Excel toolbar a $ sign will be displayed. Comments are inserted into a cell by right clicking the cell and choosing Insert Comment. Comments can be modified and deleted in the same way. To make comments visible at all times, choose Review, Show All Comments from the Excel toolbar.

Excel Basics – Formatting percents.
Another formatting option is to format a cell (or a group of cells) as 'Percent'. This is helpful if you want to display a cell value of .11 as 11% or 1.25 as 125%. The reverse is also true. If you format a cell as 'Percent' the value you enter into that cell is automatically converted to a percent. So if your shift differential for 2nd shift is 4%, and you have NOT formatted cell B18 as 'Percent' (i.e. it is formatted as 'General' or 'Number') you should enter 0.04, the numerical equivalent of 4%. If you have formatted the cell as 'Percent' you should enter 4 and Excel will automatically treat it as 0.04.

The other mark you can see on this screen shot is in the upper-left corner of several cells, for instance, in cell B19. In a worksheet, the triangle will be green and it is a warning from Excel. There are various warnings as well as specific error messages that Excel may deliver to you about the formulas you have created or the cells you have linked.

> **Excel Basics – Warning and error messages**
> In the case of an error, it will be displayed directly in the cell, such as #NUM!, which means that an incorrect number is used in the formula, or #VALUE!, that an incorrect argument or operator is used in the formula. In the case of a warning, you must click on the triangle and Excel will tell you what it is believes is wrong. In this case the warning in cell B19 reads: "The formula or function used is divided by zero or an empty cell." Since the value for AveST wage in Format Worksheet #1 or #2 has not yet been calculated, the warning message is valid. It would disappear as soon as the average straight-time wage is calculated in the linked worksheet.

Data from the Regional Medical Center

The Regional Medical Center did not provide any information on its TOTAL ANNUAL COST for shift differentials but an estimate of the cost can be made because 24 employees are normally scheduled on the second shift with a premium of $1.50 per hour worked and 14 employees are scheduled on the third shift with a premium of $2.75 per hour worked.

How many hours did those employees on second and third shifts work in the year? The overall average hours worked by the bargaining unit can be used unless there is reason to believe that shift workers have worked considerably more or less than the average. Are Productive Hours used here? The answer is a qualified yes; shift differential is paid for the hours actually worked. If shift employees at RMC also receive shift differential while on vacation, for a public holiday not worked, while on sick leave or other paid leave, the amount of the shift differential can be incorporated as part of the cost of those benefits.

Some contracts do not include shift differentials in some, or all, of these paid-but-not-worked hours. So check your contract language to determine whether to include shift differential payments.

The following screen print shows the calculation of the shift differential costs for the Regional Medical Center. The ANNUAL COST for shift differentials is $123,593, the ANNUAL COST PER EMPLOYEE is $1,287 and the AVERAGE COST PER HOUR is $0.78.

Even though only 38 employees in the bargaining unit are receiving shift differentials, the average cost of shift differentials must be expressed over the entire bargaining unit, which means dividing by the total number of employees (96) and the productive hours. For the union negotiating committee to be able to compare the shift differentials paid to these 38 employees to other contractual benefits, the cost/value needs to be expressed in this way.

The average value of shift differentials **for the 38 employees** is $3,276 per year or $1.96 per hour but this is equivalent to $.78 across the entire bargaining unit. If shift differentials were removed from the contract, all employees could receive a $.78 wage increase without any additional cost to the employer. Or if shift differentials for these 38 employees were increased by 50%, the cost to the employer would be equivalent to a $.39 wage increase for all employees. In order for the union negotiating committee to make these kinds of comparisons, it needs to know the overall cost of a benefit that applies to only some members of the bargaining unit.

	A	B	C	D	E
1	**RMC Worksheet #4 - Hourly Wage-Related Premium Payments**				
2					
11	Shift Differentials	2nd Shift	3rd Shift	Other	TOTAL SD COST
12	Flat Hourly Shift Differentials	$ 1.50	$ 2.75		
13	Number of Employees Receiving	24	14		
14	Average Number of Hours Worked	1671	1671		
15	ANNUAL COST	$ 60,157.87	$ 64,335.50		$124,493.37
16	ANNUAL COST PER EMPLOYEE				$1,296.81
17	AVERAGE COST PER HOUR				$0.78
18	Percentage Hourly Shift Differentials				
19	Average Hourly Wage				
20	Number of Employees Receiving				
21	Average Number of Hours Worked				
22	ANNUAL COST				
23	ANNUAL COST PER EMPLOYEE				
24	AVERAGE COST PER HOUR				

Other Hourly Wage Premiums

There may be other types of hourly wage differentials in a collective agreement. For instance, premiums might be paid for all work on the 6th or 7th consecutive day, regardless of the number of hours worked in previous workdays or whether they constitute hours greater than 40 in a week. These types of premium payments may be "pyramided" on

top of overtime premium payments, although they are usually not. There may be premiums for weekend work whether or not those hours of work constitute weekly overtime.

Most contracts specify premium payments for work actually performed on holidays. In many union contracts this is 1.5 (or more) times the regular rate, but in workplaces that must routinely operate on holidays, the premium is often much less. The other specific hourly wage premiums listed in Format Spreadsheet #4 is float differential which is in many health care contracts. Other collective agreements may have 'hazard pay' for certain hours of work. The union negotiating committee should carefully review the types of premium payments under its contract to understand when they apply and when they do not and how they relate to other premiums such as overtime.

As before, the union should request data from the employer on at least the Total Annual Cost for each premium and the total number of such hours paid. With those two pieces of information the union can evaluate the reliability of the data. If there are concerns about the actual application of these premium payments, the union can prepare a follow-up informational request asking for more details such as the classifications, or names of employees, who qualified for such premium payments.

Skill-Based Hourly Premiums

The last category of premiums in Format Worksheet #4 is for those that are based on skill, education or job responsibility. In health care contracts such premiums have been noted for various classification differentials (e.g. Charge Nurse, Team Leader or Head Nurse), degree differential for those employees with a B.S.N. or M.S.N. and for holding certain certifications. These three categories are listed in the worksheet and should be modified for any such skill-based premiums in your contract. For the purpose of Format Worksheet #4, only those skill-based premiums that are paid on an hourly basis are included. If these premiums are paid on an annual or semi-annual basis they can be more easily calculated in Format Worksheet #8 – Annual Payments & Allowances.

The union should request data from the employer on any skill-based premiums. Again, the minimum information might be just the number of employees who are receiving each type of skill-based premium or the employer's Total Annual Cost for each of these types of premiums. If the union has concerns about the reliability of the information or it is a seemingly inaccurate amount, additional details and a breakdown of the information can be requested as part of the negotiating process.

Data from the Regional Medical Center

As shown in the screen print below, the Regional Medical Center provided information that it paid a ½ time premium (0.5) for hours worked on holidays and that the total number of holiday hours worked was 784. The total premium payments for holidays worked is calculated as 0.5*784*AveST. From this the ANNUAL COST ($6,690.98), the ANNUAL COST PER EMPLOYEE ($69.70) and AVERAGE COST PER HOUR ($0.04) are derived.

	A	B	C	D	E
1	**RMC Worksheet #4 - Hourly Wage-Related Premium Payments**				
2					
26	Other Hourly Wage Premiums	Amount of Hourly Premium	# of Premium Hours Paid	Average ST Wage	TOTAL PREMIUM COST
27	Holiday Work Premium	0.5	784	17.07	$6,690.98
28	Weekend Work Differential				
29	Float Differential				
30	Other Wage-Related Premiums				
31	ANNUAL COST				$6,690.98
32	ANNUAL COST PER EMPLOYEE				$69.70
33	AVERAGE COST PER HOUR				$0.04

A careful examination of this screen print will reveal that rows 1 and 2 are shown and that the next row is 26. What happened to rows 3 to 25? Quite simply, they were hidden. This is a useful feature of Excel to display only certain information or when preparing to print only the most necessary data. In order to show the column headings on this worksheet but not the parts on overtime premiums and shift differentials, those rows were hidden – not eliminated – but only temporarily hidden.

Excel Basics – Hide and unhide rows and columns

It is easy to do: simply select (highlight) the rows you want to hide; then right-click and from the dropdown menu choose Hide. When you want to see those rows again, you must highlight the first row above and the first row below the hidden area, in this case rows 2 and 26, then right-click, and choose Unhide from the dropdown menu. It is also possible to hide and unhide columns by following the same steps as for rows. However, it is best to NOT hide column A. Though it can be 'unhidden' it requires several extra, more complicated steps.

Further examination of this worksheet as well as the preceding ones also shows that the TOTAL ANNUAL COST, ANNUAL COST PER EMPLOYEE AND AVERAGE COST PER HOUR have been consistently calculated (and displayed) in cells in column E. While this certainly is not essential in constructing a series of linked worksheets there is some value in maintaining a consistent format within a workbook. That way, when certain data is linked, for example to a summary page, it is easier to find its location.

Chapter 6 – Pay for Non-Work Time

THERE ARE VARIOUS benefits in a union contract requiring payments for non-work time. The principal ones are pay during annual vacation and pay for holidays. Other types of paid leave such as sickness, bereavement, serving on a jury or performing union duties are also quite common.

Costing some of these benefits is often problematic in that they can be highly variable over the course of several years. Particularly in smaller bargaining units, the costs for bereavement leave or jury duty leave could vary considerably from year to year. Overall though, the costs of these leaves are usually quite small.

The more costly benefits are for vacations and paid holidays because typically all members of the bargaining unit are entitled to the benefit and all employees usually use their right to holidays with pay and annual vacation leave. Or in some circumstances employees are paid an equivalent amount if they do not take some part of their vacation leave.

Holidays

Costing holidays not worked is fairly straightforward. An employee not working on a holiday is paid for his or her regularly scheduled hours (8 or 10 or 12) and is paid at the regular rate of pay for those hours not worked. If that one employee does not work any of the designated contractual holidays during the course of the year, the cost to the employer is the number of paid holidays times the regularly scheduled hours times the employee's regular rate of pay.

However, there are several caveats to consider: what if an employee does not work the scheduled day before or after the holiday? In some contracts the employee is not entitled to holiday pay. What is that employee's regular rate of pay? Does it include shift differential? Does it include other hourly or skill-based differentials? Only a careful review of the contract will reveal how holidays that are not worked are actually compensated.

In terms of calculating pay for those employees who do actually work the holiday the costs (benefits) of them working on a holiday should be captured as a premium payment for working on a holiday. This was covered in Chapter 5.

An easy way to calculate the cost of holidays per employee is to multiply the number of contractual holidays per year times the number of hours paid for each holiday not worked times the hourly rate paid for the holiday. Because we can assume that employees in all classifications who are eligible to take holidays will do so, we can accurately use the average hourly wage rate for this variable.

However, if shift differentials or other hourly premiums are included as part of holiday pay, the average straight-time rate should be adjusted to include these premiums. It is reasonable to assume that the average hourly cost of shift differentials is an accurate amount to add to the average straight-time wage rate for the purpose of estimating the additional cost of paid holidays for shift employees. Likewise, the average cost of any other hourly premiums that are included in holiday pay can be added to the average straight-time wage rate.

FORMAT WORKSHEET #5

	A	B	C	D	E
1	Format Worksheet #5 - Pay for Non-Work Time				
2					
3	Holidays				
4	Number of Paid Holidays	Hours Paid for Each Holiday	Rate Paid for Each Holiday	COST PER EMPLOYEE	AVERAGE COST PER HOUR
5			=AveST+'Hourly W'	=A5*B5*C5	
6	Holiday Hours Paid/Not Worked:				
7	ANNUAL COST	=D5*TotEmp			
8	AVERAGE COST PER HOUR				=B7/PHrs

The screen print above shows the formulas that are in the format worksheet for the section on holidays. The column headings in this worksheet are also slightly different than in the previous ones but again column E is designated for capturing the AVERAGE COST PER HOUR.

The number of paid holidays is entered in cell A5. The number of hours paid for each holiday is entered in cell B5. To include shift differentials to the holiday pay the average straight-time wage is added with the average cost of shift differentials from cell E24 of the previous worksheet (the formula is in cell C5). The COST PER EMPLOYEE is the product of cells A5, B5 and C5.

The ANNUAL COST is calculated by multiplying by the number of employees who are entitled to paid holidays. If there are certain members of the bargaining unit who are excluded from receiving all or some paid holidays, such as probationary employees or per diem employees, do not include them in the calculation. Rather than using TotEmp, an adjusted number of employees can be entered. The AVERAGE COST PER HOUR is calculated by dividing cell B7 by the number of productive hours.

An alternative method is to request information from the employer on the annual cost for holiday pay, enter that in cell B7 and then calculate the AVERAGE COST PER HOUR.

Data from the Regional Medical Center

The RMC did not supply any information on the total cost for holidays paid and not worked. The contract specifies 10 holidays per year for all employees, including part-time employees working 30 hours per week. The contract also states that employees who work on a paid holiday will receive a premium payment and will be provided an alternate day off so it can be assumed that all employees are paid for all 10 holidays. RMC shift employees receive their differential premium on holidays. The AVERAGE COST PER HOUR is $0.85.

	A	B	C	D	E
1	**RMC Worksheet #5 - Pay for Non-Work Time**				
2					
3	Holidays				
4	Number of Paid Holidays	Hours Paid for Each Holiday	Rate Paid for Each Holiday	COST PER EMPLOYEE	AVERAGE COST PER HOUR
5	10	8.0	$17.84	$1,427.59	
6	Holiday Hours Paid/Not Worked:	7,680			
7	ANNUAL COST	$137,048.62			
8	AVERAGE COST PER HOUR				$0.85

Personal Days

The costs associated with personal days (i.e. days off with pay that can be taken when employees choose) can be calculated in the same manner as paid holidays, especially if the assumption can be made that all employees will take their full allotment of personal days off. However, it is important to know the rate employees are paid for personal days. Does it include shift differentials or any other hourly-wage related premiums or is it based solely on employees' base wage rate?

For both paid holidays and paid personal days, the union negotiating committee should request from the employer the total annual cost for each benefit. That can be used as the basis for calculating an average hourly cost for the bargaining unit or it can be compared to the calculated estimates for the purpose of double checking.

Data from the Regional Medical Center

The Regional Medical Center did not provide any information on the number of hours of paid personal leave or its total annual cost. The contract specifies that full-time employees receive 3 days per year and part-time employees receive 2 days per year. Note from the screen print below that the Format Worksheet has been slightly modified by adding an additional row so that the number of personal days can be calculated for both full-time and part-time employees. Note further that since there is a significant difference in the average straight-time wage between these two groups of employees ($18.72 for full-time; $15.11 for part-time), those average wage rates are used in this worksheet by naming cells E98 and E99 in RMC Worksheet #2 as AveFT (average wage for full-time employees) and AvePT (average wage for part-time employees) and using those named cells here in cells C12 and C13.

The AVERAGE COST PER HOUR for personal days in the RMC contract is $0.21.

	A	B	C	D	E
1	**RMC Worksheet #5 - Pay for Non-Work Time**				
2					
10	Personal Days				
11	Number of Paid Personal Days	Hours Paid for Each Personal Day	Rate Paid for Each Leave Day	COST PER EMPLOYEE	AVERAGE COST PER HOUR
12	3 for F-T Employees	8	$18.72	$449.34	
13	2 for P-T Employees	8	$15.11	$241.84	
14	Annual Personal Hours Paid	1,952			
15	ANNUAL COST			$34,006.20	
16	AVERAGE COST PER HOUR				$0.21

Sick Leave

It is possible for a union negotiating committee to make only rough estimates of the costs of sick leave by guessing at usage (days per year) and then calculating costs based on the average hourly wage and the number of employees. This is one of those contractual benefits for which the union must specifically request the ANNUAL COST from the employer. Certain types of sick leave usage data might also be requested from the employer. Once the employer has supplied the ANNUAL COST, the same methodology and formulas for calculating the COST PER EMPLOYEE and the AVERAGE COST PER HOUR are used.

Calculating the average number of hours of sick leave (by dividing the total cost by the average hourly wage) and then calculating the average number of sick leave hours per employee should assist the union in determining the reasonableness of the information from the employer. If there are concerns or controversies around sick leave the union should certainly make follow-up informational requests during the course of bargaining.

Data from the Regional Medical Center

The Regional Medical Center provided information that its total costs for sick leave in the year ending October 31, 2008 was $62,720. As shown in the screen print below, this ANNUAL COST was divided by the average hourly wage to calculate that 3,675 hours of sick leave were paid, about 460 days, or an average of just less than 5 days per employee over the last year. This seems like a reasonable number in the absence of contrary information. Following the standard methodology, the COST PER EMPLOYEE for the previous year was $653.33 and the AVERAGE COST PER HOUR was $0.39.

	A	B	C	D	E
1	RMC Worksheet #5 - Pay for Non-Work Time				
2					
18	Sick Leave				
19	Annual Hours of Sick Leave Paid	3,675			
20	ANNUAL COST	$62,720.00			
21	COST PER EMPLOYEE			$653.33	
22	AVERAGE COST PER HOUR				$0.39
23					
24	Bereavement Leave				
25	Annual Hours of Bereavement Paid	202			
26	ANNUAL COST	$3,456.00			
27	COST PER EMPLOYEE			$36.00	
28	AVERAGE COST PER HOUR				$0.02

Bereavement Leaves, Jury Duty Leaves and Leaves for Union Business

Bereavement leaves and jury duty leaves fall into the category of benefits/costs that can be highly variable from year to year. Paid leaves for union business might have more uniform cost over the years but could be subject to certain spikes depending on the contractual obligation of the employer (e.g. if paid leave is provided for union representatives to attend union conventions or to participate as members of the union negotiating committee).

For all three contractual benefits it is best to ask the employer to supply information on the ANNUAL COST. As shown above, the Regional Medical Center said that its total cost for bereavement leaves in the previous year was $3,456 and hence the AVERAGE COST PER HOUR was $0.02.

The Regional Medical Center contract had no provisions for jury duty leave or leave for union business. In the Format Worksheet, the formulas for calculating COST PER EMPLOYEE and AVERAGE COST PER HOUR are included.

Severance Pay

Severance pay of one type or another is included in many contracts. It certainly fits within the category of pay for time not worked, albeit in a macabre way. The union may be able to make a rough estimate of cost based on the number of separations in a year. But this is another benefit where getting the total cost from the employer for the previous year or several years is most useful.

Chapter 7 – Vacations

THE UNION NEGOTIATING committee should request the ANNUAL COST for vacations from the employer. Usually it is also helpful to have a breakdown of costs for each 'vacation eligibility period' (i.e. the number of employees entitled to various levels of vacation) so that the union negotiating committee can estimate the costs of improving the vacation schedule by either adding additional days or weeks to one or more eligibility periods in the schedule or by reducing the number of years required for eligibility for defined periods of vacation.

FORMAT WORKSHEET #6

	A	B	C	D	E
1	**Format Worksheet #6 -Vacation Pay**				
2					
3	Number of Days or Weeks of Vacation	Number of Hours Paid	Number of Eligible Employees	Vacation Pay Rate	SUBTOTAL COST
4					
5					
6					
7					
8					
9	Total Hours of Paid Vacation:				
10	ANNUAL COST				
11	ANNUAL COST PER EMPLOYEE				
12	AVERAGE COST PER HOUR				

This worksheet has no pre-entered formulas. There are many ways to 'skin the cat' and the method you use will depend on how your contract provisions on vacations are structured (in days, weeks or some other way), whether some employees receive pro-rata vacations (for instance, part-time employees or employees with less than one year of service) and at what rate vacations are paid (at base wage, or including shift differentials, overtime, etc.). The bottom line is to get to is cell E12 with the costs of vacations expressed as an AVERAGE COST PER HOUR.

In Column A, data on the number of days or weeks of vacation eligibility is entered. If there is some combination like 2 weeks after 3 years of service and then 2 weeks plus 3 days after five weeks of service, it is easier to convert everything to days of vacation eligibility. The format worksheet has five rows for five defined vacation eligibility periods but additional rows can be easily added if your contract has more eligibility periods.

In column B, the number of hours paid for each eligibility period is calculated based on 8 hours for each day or 40 hours for each week of vacation. If employees work 10 hour shifts and are paid vacation pay on this basis, it can be entered appropriately here. The formula in column B4 would generally be =A4*40 if A4 is expressed in weeks and =A4*8 if A4 is expressed in days. If the number of weeks/days for each period is constant, which is usually the case, this formula can then be inserted down column B by copying and pasting or by clicking and dragging the formula from cell B4, using the Auto Fill handle.

In column D, the appropriate pay rate for each vacation hour is entered. In many cases the average straight-time wage rate can be used. However, some contracts specify that shift differentials are included in the vacation rate; others include other hourly differentials; and still others include overtime work. Sometimes, the latter is accomplished by making vacation pay some proportion of annual earnings. A common formula is 2% of annual earnings for each week of vacation eligibility. This would include all premiums and differentials that an employee had earned over the course of the (previous) year. A fairly accurate estimate of these annual earnings can be constructed by adding the average hourly costs for shift differentials (and other hourly wage-based premiums) and overtime to the average straight-time hourly wage as well as, perhaps, the average cost of pay for time not worked.

A final consideration on vacation pay is whether employees who are eligible for a greater number of weeks of vacation have a higher average wage rate than those with less vacation. This is quite possible, particularly in contracts with many steps in a wage progression that extends over a long time period. But the impact on the accuracy of the calculated estimate is not likely to be too great. The way to tell is to compare the TOTAL ANNUAL COST from the worksheet with an annual cost figure obtained from the employer.

In column C, the number of employees eligible for each period of vacation entitlement is entered. This reflects a certain point in time, with the understanding that employees may be moving to higher periods of eligibility on their anniversary dates or at other fixed dates within the calendar year. Except for the smallest bargaining units, it makes sense to enter information from your bargaining unit's seniority list into an Excel worksheet so that you can easily break down the unit into categories of years of service. Note that the information received from the Regional Medical Center with the number of full-time and part-time employees and years of service is formatted in three columns in Worksheet #10 (Data from the Employer). From such information on a worksheet it is very simple to determine how many employees are currently in each vacation eligibility category and to pursue the impact of various 'what if' scenarios with changed vacation eligibility.

Care should be taken to exclude any bargaining unit employees who are not eligible for *any* vacation if they are a significant part of the bargaining unit. These may be probationary employees or contingent employees or even part-time employees. If part-time employees are eligible for some proportion of vacation pay, they can be included in this format based on the amount of vacation to which they are eligible or additional rows can be added to the spreadsheet specifically to distinguish between the part-time and full-time employees.

Data from the Regional Medical Center

Employees at the Regional Medical Center receive 2 weeks' vacation if they have less than 8 years of service; 3 weeks between 8 years and less than 15 years; 4 weeks at 15 years and less than 25; and 5 weeks at 25 years. Part-time employees receive pro-rata vacation benefits, meaning that they receive 30 hours pay for each week of vacation rather than 40. In all cases, vacation is paid at an employee's straight-time wage rate without inclusion of any additional premium payments.

	A	B	C	D	E
1	**RMC Worksheet #6 -Vacation Pay**				
2					
3	Number of Days or Weeks of Vacation	Number of Hours Paid	Number of Eligible Employees	Vacation Pay Rate	SUBTOTAL COST
4	**Full-time employees**				
5	2	80	25		
6	3	120	19		
7	4	160	8		
8	5	200	0		
9	**Part-time employees**				
10	2	60	21		
11	3	90	18		
12	4	120	5		
13	5	150	0		
14	Total Hours of Paid Vacation:		9040	$17.07	
15	ANNUAL COST			$154,302.23	
16	ANNUAL COST PER EMPLOYEE				$1,607.31
17	AVERAGE COST PER HOUR				$0.96

Because part-time employees receive only pro-rata vacation pay, it seems worthwhile to separate Worksheet #6 into rows with separate sections for full-time and part-time employees. And it is easy to calculate the number of part-time and full-time employees in each vacation eligibility category from the data supplied from the RMC because it is in a spreadsheet format (see the Data from the Employer worksheet for the formulas to sum the number of employees in each category). Cells C5 – C8 and C10 – C13 can be simply linked to the Data from the Employer worksheet. Note that in this worksheet SUBTOTAL COSTS were not calculated for each category of vacation eligibility; rather the total number of vacation hours was calculated (9,040) and then the assumed-to-be-accurate vacation pay rate of $17.07 (the average straight-time rate) was multiplied times those hours to arrive at the ANNUAL COST. The AVERAGE COST PER HOUR for vacations at the RMC is $0.96. This is the cost that will be used through the remainder of the manual. However, for illustration purposes an additional calculation is made costing vacations separately for full-time and part-time employees.

Since full-time employees are paid, on average, more than part-time employees perhaps different average wage rates should be used for the two groups. It is not difficult to modify the worksheet to do so; the number of vacation hours must be calculated separately for each group, and then coupled with the average straight-time hourly rates for each group which were already named as AveFT and AvePT.

It is not necessary to construct an entirely new spreadsheet to do this type of "what if" scenario. Simply copy the cells (and usually formats and formulas) to another part of the same worksheet, make the necessary modifications and quickly the second scenario is created.

Below is RMC Worksheet #6a which was created on the same worksheet by copying the existing cells from A1 to E17 by using the normal copy command, clicking in cell A19 and pasting all those cells. **A big caution here!** Since cells C5 – C8 and C10 – C13 were linked to cells in column F in the 'Data from the Employer' worksheet, Excel can be a little "too smart" because it will automatically paste 'corresponding' cells from column F of that worksheet into Worksheet #6a. Fortunately, Excel has several options that can be used when pasting cells that you have copied. In this case, the reference link itself should not be copied; rather the Paste Special command is chosen and then paste '*values*'.

RMC Worksheet #6a - Vacation Pay

	Number of Days or Weeks of Vacation	Number of Hours Paid	Number of Eligible Employees	Vacation Pay Rate	SUBTOTAL COST
Full-time employees					
	2	80	25		
	3	120	19		
	4	160	8		
	5	200	0		
	Subtotal		5560	$18.72	$104,095.95
Part-time employees					
	2	60	21		
	3	90	18		
	4	120	5		
	5	150	0		
	Subtotal		3480	$15.11	$52,599.29
Total Hours of Paid Vacation:			9040		
ANNUAL COST				$156,695.24	
ANNUAL COST PER EMPLOYEE					$1,632.24
AVERAGE COST PER HOUR					$0.98

As shown above, SUBTOTAL COSTS are calculated separately for full-time and part-time employees based on their respective average straight-time wage rates. The AVERAGE COST PER HOUR is now $0.98, rather than $0.96 as in RMC Worksheet #6.

Chapter 8 – Health/Dental/Life/Disability Insurance

IN MOST UNION contracts, all forms of insurance, including health, dental, group life and short-term disability insurance, sometimes called sickness and accident benefits are paid by the employer as a monthly premium to an insurer or health-care provider. While the employer usually makes the actual premium payments, in the case of health care, the costs are increasingly shared by the employees.

If all employees are covered under the same health care plan and the employer pays the entire premium for coverage, the calculation of ANNUAL COST for health insurance is quite straightforward. However, it is common for employees to have choices among several types of health insurance plans (traditional indemnity plans, HMO and PPO plans) and/or for coverage to be based on an employee's family status or number of dependents. There are often similar variables for group dental insurance plans.

Group life insurance benefits (and accidental death and dismemberment (AD&D) insurance) varies as well, usually related in some way to the employees' earnings level. For example, it might be equivalent to some factor times annual earnings rather than a flat amount of life insurance for all employees. Regardless, the employer most likely pays a monthly premium for life insurance (or the share of monthly life insurance purchased by the employer if employees have the option to supplement the level of life insurance by purchasing additional amounts themselves).

Short-term disability insurance is commonly covered through an insurance company although larger employers sometimes decide to 'self-insure' these benefits. It is common for short-term disability insurance to be based on replacement of some proportion of an employee's wages, for instance 60 percent of regular wages. The plans have varying criteria for eligibility and the commencement of benefits (after first day of accident and fifth day of illness, for example). If the employer purchases insurance for this benefit, there is probably a monthly premium. If the employer self-insures, it knows its total annual cost.

Health Insurance

FORMAT WORKSHEET #7

Format Worksheet #7, below, shows a method for capturing cost data for health insurance plans. Column A lists three types of plans (an indemnity plan, a PPO plan and a HMO plan) and three types of coverage based on the employee's family status (single, family and single + 1 dependent). This can be modified, of course, to reflect the structure of health insurance plans in your collective agreement by adding or eliminating categories of family status or other types of plans.

	A	B	C	D	E	F
1	Format Worksheet #7 - Health/Life/Disability Insurance					
2						
3	Type of Health Coverage	Number of Enrolled EEs	EE's Monthly Premium	ER's Monthly Premium	TOTAL Monthly Premium	TOTAL ANNUAL COST
4	Indemnity Plan					
5	Single Employee			=E5-C5		=B5*E5*12
6	Family			=E6-C6		=B6*E6*12
7	Single + 1 Dependent			=E7-C7		=B7*E7*12
8	PPO Plan					
9	Single Employee					
10	Family					
11	Single + 1 Dependent					
12	HMO Plan					
13	Single Employee					
14	Family					
15	Single + 1 Dependent					
16	EMPLOYER'S TOTAL MONTHLY COST			=(B5*D5+B6*D6+B7*D7)		
17	EMPLOYER'S ANNUAL COST			=D16*12		
18	ANNUAL COST PER EMPLOYEE			=D17/TotEmp		
19	AVERAGE COST PER HOUR			=D18/PHrs		
20						
21	Employees' Total Monthly Contributions		=(B5*C5+B6*C6+B7*C7)			
22	Employees' Annual Contributions		=C21*12			
23	Average Cost Per Employee Contributing					
24	Average Employee Contribution Per Hour		=C23/PHrs			
25	TOTAL ANNUAL COST				=D17+C22	=SUM(F5:F24)

Note on row 23 (D column): Here we want to divide only by the number of employees who are actually making contributions if that is not the entire bargaining unit.

For each type of plan, data is added on the number of employees enrolled in that plan, the total monthly premium and the employees' monthly premium, if any. This worksheet has been formatted so that the employer's monthly premium is the total monthly premium minus the employee's monthly premium. Though it is not essential to retain this formula for calculating the employer's premium, this format might have some usefulness to a union negotiating committee if employees currently pay part of the premium and the committee wants to examine some 'what if' scenarios with reduced levels of contributions by employees. In this format, the data that must be entered are the total monthly premium for each plan and family status, the employees' contribution (if it is zero that should be entered) and the number of employees who are enrolled in that particular plan and family category.

The formulas are shown here as if there is only an indemnity plan. The total annual cost for each sub grouping of the indemnity plan is the number of employees enrolled in that plan times the total monthly premium times 12 months. The same formulas can be copied into the areas for the PPO and HMO plans if such plans are available.

The employer's total monthly cost is calculated by multiplying the number of employees in each category times the employer's monthly premium cost. If a collective agreement had all three types of plans the formula shown as =(B5*D5+B6*D6+B7*D7) needs to be extended further by including +(B9*D9+B10*D10+B11*D11), etc. The employer's total annual cost is D16 times 12 months and the ANNUAL COST PER EMPLOYEE and the AVERAGE COST PER HOUR are calculated by dividing by TotEmp and then PHrs.

Since some or all of the employees may be paying a part of the cost of health insurance the Format Worksheet has an area for capturing their total monthly premiums and annual contributions towards health insurance (cells C21 and C22). The same type of formula is constructed for the monthly employee contributions and the total annual contributions by employees are calculated by multiplying by 12. However, the AVERAGE ANNUAL COST PER EMPLOYEE should not be based on the total number of employees but rather only on the number of employees who are paying some portion of the health insurance – the Average Cost per Employee Contributing. Of course, if all employees are paying something towards health insurance TotEmp can be used. Lastly, the average hourly cost for those employees who are making health insurance contributions can be calculated. The union may also want to calculate the AVERAGE COST PER HOUR based on the entire bargaining unit.

The final parts of this Format Worksheet are the total costs for health insurance on the part of the employer and employees. Column F has the total cost for each type of plan and its family categories and an AutoSum is entered in cell F25. As a double check the total annual cost is also calculated as the sum of the employer's total annual cost (cell D17) and the employees' annual contributions (cell C25).

The union negotiating committee must request from the employer a breakdown of the monthly premium cost for each type of plan and each type of coverage and a count of the number of employees who have elected each plan/coverage.

Data from the Regional Medical Center

The Regional Medical Center has both a traditional indemnity plan and a HMO plan and each plan has categories for single (employee) coverage, family coverage, and single + one dependent. Full-time employees choosing to cover only themselves with either the indemnity plan or the HMO plan do not pay any portion of the premium. Employees choosing family coverage or single + one dependent pay part of the premium and part-time employees pay more than full-time employees for each category of coverage. In all, there are twelve different amounts that employees pay depending on the plan they choose, their work status and their family status.

Only 81 of the medical center's 96 employees are enrolled in one of the health care plans. All full-time employees chose to do so but 15 of the 44 part-time employees do not have health insurance coverage through the medical center, presumably because they have coverage under a spouse's plan or chose not to enroll, perhaps because of the cost. In order to capture the different costs for part-time employees, three additional rows for the indemnity plan and for the HMO plan were inserted into the Format Worksheet.

As shown in the following screen shot, the employer's TOTAL ANNUAL COST for health insurance is $389,977.44 and its AVERAGE COST PER HOUR is $2.43. Employees contributed a total of $66,120 for health insurance and the average cost per hour for the 63 employees who are making contributions is $0.61. Total health insurance costs are $456,097.

	A	B	C	D	E	F
1	**RMC Worksheet #7 - Health/Life/Disability Insurance**					
2						
3	**Type of Health Coverage**	Number of Enrolled Employees	Employee's Monthly Premium	Employer's Monthly Premium	TOTAL Monthly Premium	TOTAL ANNUAL COST
4	**Indemnity Plan**					
5	Single Employee	10	$0.00	$327.40	$327.40	$39,288.00
6	Family	6	$90.00	$720.62	$810.62	$58,364.64
7	Single + 1 Dependent	4	$60.00	$542.90	$602.90	$28,939.20
8	P-T Single Employee	6	$90.00	$237.40	$327.40	$23,572.80
9	P-T Family	2	$180.00	$630.62	$810.62	$19,454.88
10	P-T Single + 1 Dependent	3	$120.00	$482.90	$602.90	$21,704.40
11	**PPO Plan**					
12	Single Employee					
13	Family					
14	Single + 1 Dependent					
15	**HMO Plan**					
16	Single Employee	8	$0.00	$247.74	$247.74	$23,783.04
17	Family	12	$70.00	$491.62	$561.62	$80,873.28
18	Single + 1 Dependent	12	$50.00	$376.68	$426.68	$61,441.92
19	P-T Single Employee	3	$70.00	$177.74	$247.74	$8,918.64
20	P-T Family	8	$140.00	$421.62	$561.62	$53,915.52
21	P-T Single + 1 Dependent	7	$100.00	$326.68	$426.68	$35,841.12
22	EMPLOYER'S TOTAL MONTHLY COST			$32,498.12		
23	EMPLOYER'S ANNUAL COST			$389,977.44		
24	ANNUAL COST PER EMPLOYEE			$4,062.27		
25	AVERAGE COST PER HOUR			$2.43		
26	Enrolled employees	81				
27	Employees' Total Monthly Contributions		$5,510.00			
28	Employees' Annual Contributions		$66,120.00			
29	Average Cost Per Employee Contributing		$1,049.52			
30	Average Employee Contribution Per Hour		$0.63			
31	Total Cost for Health Insurance				$456,097.44	$456,097.44

Dental Insurance

Costing dental insurance may not be as complicated as health insurance but there are several variables that may need to be included in the worksheet. Coverage may be based on an employee's family status, contributions may be required by some or all employees and some employees may not be covered, for instance part-time employees or employees with less than one year of service.

The dental insurance part of the Format Worksheet has only one insurance plan but has three categories for single employee, family and single + one dependent. It is constructed in the same way as for health insurance, permitting calculation of premiums paid by employees if they are required. Similarly, the formula for the employer's premium is the total premium minus the employee's premium, if any. If the employer pays the entire premium, the data to be entered are the number of enrolled employees, the total monthly premium and zero for the employees' share of the premium. The employer's ANNUAL COST is the monthly premium rate times 12 times the number of covered employees. If coverage is not made available to new employees for a certain period, for instance 6 months or 12 months, this can generally be ignored unless there are a substantial number of new employees. The remaining formulas in the Format Worksheet follow the same methodology as for health insurance.

	A	B	C	D	E	F
1	Format Worksheet #7 - Health/Life/Disability Insurance					
3	Type of Health Coverage	Number of Enrolled EEs	EE's Monthly Premium	ER's Monthly Premium	TOTAL Monthly Premium	TOTAL ANNUAL COST
27	Dental Insurance					
28	Single Employee			=E28-C28		=E28*12
29	Single + 1 Dependent			=E29-C29		=E29*12
30	Family			=E30-C30		=E30*12
31	EMPLOYER'S TOTAL MONTHLY COST			=B28*D28+B29*D29+B30*D30		
32	EMPLOYER'S ANNUAL COST			=D31*12		
33	ANNUAL COST PER EMPLOYEE			=D32/TotEmp		
34	AVERAGE COST PER HOUR			=D33/PHrs		
35						
36	Employees' Total Monthly Contributions		=B28*C28+B29*C29+B30*C30			
37	Employees' Annual Contributions		=C36*12			
38	Contribution Per Employee Contributing					
39	Average Employee Contribution Per Hour		=C38/PHrs			
40	TOTAL ANNUAL COST				=D32+C37	=SUM(F28:F39)

Data from the Regional Medical Center

The Regional Medical Center covers all of its employees, full-time and part-time, with the same dental plan, regardless of family status and the employer pays the entire premium cost, $101.00 per month per employee. This part of the worksheet for the medical center is, therefore, quite simple.

	A	B	C	D	E	F
1	**RMC Worksheet #7 - Health/Life/Disability Insurance**					
3	Type of Health Coverage	Number of Enrolled Employees	Employee's Monthly Premium	Employer's Monthly Premium	TOTAL Monthly Premium	TOTAL ANNUAL COST
34	Dental Insurance					
35	Single Employee					
36	Single + 1 Dependent					
37	Family					
38	EMPLOYER'S TOTAL MONTHLY COST	96	$0.00	$101.00	$101.00	$9,696.00
39	EMPLOYER'S ANNUAL COST					$116,352.00
40	ANNUAL COST PER EMPLOYEE					$1,212.00
41	AVERAGE COST PER HOUR					$0.73

Life Insurance

Life insurance, usually paid on a monthly-premium basis, is often non-contributory for employees, but sometimes employees are permitted to buy additional amounts of coverage at their own cost. The union negotiating committee should request from the employer its monthly premium cost for life insurance or the ANNUAL COST.

Note that the life insurance section of Worksheet #7 contains two rows, one titled "Flat Amount Coverage" and the other "Coverage Dependent on Income." This is a minor matter but does deserve some explanation. A flat amount means an identical amount of life insurance for all employees regardless of classification or annual earnings. Coverage dependent on income means life insurance that is in some way related to an employee's earnings. Sometimes this is expressed as equivalent to an employee's wage rate multiplied times 2,080 hours; sometime annual earnings rounded to the nearest thousand or even double an employee's annual earnings. For either type of life insurance coverage it is likely that the employer is paying a specific monthly premium to an insurance company which is adjusted on a periodic basis, usually annually.

The minor difference is that the premium for the latter type of life insurance (based on earnings) is likely to increase annually as wages increase. This type of life insurance could then, typically, be included as a fringe benefit that has a "roll-up" cost (see Chapter 9 for a more complete explanation of this concept). Overall, the cost for life insurance for a typical bargaining unit is quite small in comparison to other benefits because the premiums are based on the fact that this is a working-age population, presumably in good health. Of course, bargaining units with older average ages will typically have higher life insurance costs than those with younger average ages.

Many collective agreements also include insurance for accidental death and dismemberment which is often underwritten by the same insurance company which provides the life insurance. Additional rows can be added to the worksheet for AD&D or it can be calculated as part of life insurance.

Short-Term Disability/Sickness and Accident Benefits

This benefit covers non-occupational injuries or illnesses and typically provides replacement income after certain waiting periods, for instance, after the first day of accident and after the 7th day of illness. It is usually supplemental to any sick leave provisions in the contract which will cover a first day of illness at full wages but with a numerical limit on the number of days that can be used each year. Often S&A provides coverage for up to 52 weeks but in some collective agreements it can be for as short as 13 weeks.

Typically, an employer pays a monthly premium for coverage from an insurer. Two rows are included in the Format Worksheet based on whether there is a flat benefit amount per week (regardless of job classification) or whether the weekly benefit amount is based on some proportion of an employee's wage rate or regular earnings (for example, 60% of regular weekly earnings). The latter type of coverage could be included in "roll-up" costs.

The union negotiating committee should request from the employer its monthly premium cost for short-term disability/S&A benefits or its ANNUAL COST.

Larger employers usually have less risk than smaller employers of a significant proportion of their employees becoming incapacitated for short periods (e.g., when four employees traveling together to work are in an accident and are incapacitated for 3 months), and choose to 'self-insure' short-term disability benefits, paying the costs from their own account rather than purchasing insurance. In these cases, the union negotiating committee should request the employer's total annual cost for the previous year, and perhaps for several years, as the usage of this benefit could be quite variable over several years.

	A	B	C	D	E	F
1	**Format Worksheet #7 - Health/Life/Disability Insurance**					
2						
3	Type of Health Coverage	Number of Enrolled EEs	EE's Monthly Premium	ER's Monthly Premium	TOTAL Monthly Premium	TOTAL ANNUAL COST
42	Life Insurance					
43	Flat Amount Coverage			=E43-C43		=B43*D43*12
44	Coverage Dependent on Income					
45	ANNUAL COST PER EMPLOYEE					=F43/TotEmp
46	AVERAGE COST PER HOUR					=F45/PHrs
47						
48	Short-Term Disability/S&A Benefits					
49	Flat Amount Coverage			=E49-C49		=B49*D49*12
50	Coverage Dependent on Income					
51	ANNUAL COST PER EMPLOYEE					=F49/TotEmp
52	AVERAGE COST PER HOUR					=F51/PHrs
53						
54	Other Insurance Coverage					

The Format Worksheet for life insurance and short-term disability follows the previous pattern and shows the employer's monthly premium to be the total monthly premium minus the employee's monthly premium. However, it is rare for employees to pay any part of the cost for these benefits. Likewise, though there is a formula for calculating annual cost based on the number of employees times the employer's monthly premium times 12 months, it is just as common to get the employer's total annual cost for life insurance and short-term disability and put that figure in cells F43 and F49, respectively. Either way, from the TOTAL ANNUAL COSTS, the ANNUAL COST PER EMPLOYEE and the AVERAGE COST PER HOUR can be calculated.

Data from the Regional Medical Center

The Regional Medical Center provided information that its monthly premium cost for life insurance for all employees is $26.50 per month. Because the Regional Medical Center contract is in New Jersey, employees are covered by one of the few state-based non-occupational sickness and accident benefit programs which means there is no provision in their collective agreement and no contractual cost. As shown below, the TOTAL ANNUAL COST for life insurance is $28,224 and the AVERAGE COST PER HOUR is $0.18.

	A	B	C	D	E	F
1	**RMC Worksheet #7 - Health/Life/Disability Insurance**					
3	Type of Health Coverage	Number of Enrolled Employees	Employee's Monthly Premium	Employer's Monthly Premium	TOTAL Monthly Premium	TOTAL ANNUAL COST
48	Life Insurance					
49	Flat Amount Coverage	96	$0.00	$24.50	$2,352.00	$28,224.00
50	Coverage Dependent on Income					
51	ANNUAL COST PER EMPLOYEE					$294.00
52	AVERAGE COST PER HOUR					$0.18
53						
54	Short-Term Disability/S&A Benefits					
55	Flat Amount Coverage					
56	Coverage Dependent on Income					
57	ANNUAL COST PER EMPLOYEE					
58	AVERAGE COST PER HOUR					

Other Insurance Coverage

There may be separate coverage of prescription drugs or vision care programs that are distinct from the health care plan. If so, a similar format based on monthly premiums and number of covered employees can be used or the employer's total annual cost can be requested.

Chapter 9 – Annual Payments and Allowances

SOME BENEFITS – like uniform or clothing allowances, reimbursements for tuition, allowances for purchasing or replacing tools, lump sums for acquiring certain certifications or skills, or longevity bonuses to employees who have reached the top of their progression – are paid by the employer on an annual or irregular basis. The union negotiating committee should request the employer's annual costs for these benefits. These types of benefits will usually have a low cost.

There are other benefits with more significant costs. Principal among these are retirement plans whether they are defined-benefit plans, defined-contribution plans or 401(k) plans in which the employer matches or otherwise contributes to employees' personal pension savings.

Retirement Plans

Defined-benefit plans require annual or more frequent reviews by an actuary. The trustees of the plan are responsible for investment decisions and administration of the plan in accordance with the terms of a separate pension document.

Based on the actuarial evaluation and the past investment returns of the pension fund, and in accordance with regulations under the Employee Retirement Income Security Act (ERISA), the employer is required to make a contribution to the pension fund to keep the plan actuarially sound. This amount, usually paid annually, is the key figure that the union should request from the employer. Because of the variability of that amount caused by high investment gains in some years and the large investment losses experienced in the most recent past, the union should have information on the employer's contribution to the defined-benefit plan over a series of years.

Defined-contribution plans or contributions to a multi-employer plan in which a contribution rate is based on an hourly amount are obviously quite easy to calculate on the basis of AVERAGE COST PER HOUR although here the union committee should carefully examine on which hours the contribution is made. Does it include overtime hours (usually, but the contribution is rarely paid at a premium rate); does it include hours paid but not worked such as holidays and vacations (again, usually it does); does it include hours when an employee is on a leave for short-term disability or maternity/parental leave?

Supplemental Unemployment Benefits

Another type of benefit which has been included in this category is Supplemental Unemployment Benefits (SUB pay) which has been negotiated in some industries to supplement state-based unemployment compensation. Plan designs vary considerably as to when benefits are paid and for how long. The union should request the annual amount paid in SUB and/or the amount that the employer contributed to the SUB fund.

FORMAT WORKSHEET #8

Format Worksheet #8 is designed to enter the cost of benefits paid by the employer on an annual basis. Once the union negotiating committee has requested and obtained that information, the committee should analyze it for reasonableness and then request any underlying data on usage. This information is entered as the ANNUAL COST and then is converted to a COST PER EMPLOYEE and to an AVERAGE COST PER HOUR.

	A	B	C	D	E
1	Format Worksheet #8 - Annual Payments & Allowances				
2			Annual Cost	Cost Per Employee	Average Cost Per Hour
3	Uniforms/Clothing Allowances				
4	ANNUAL COST				
5	COST PER EMPLOYEE			=C4/TotEmp	
6	AVERAGE COST PER HOUR				=D5/PHrs
7					
8	Tool Allowance/Tool Replacement Costs				
9	ANNUAL COST				
10	COST PER EMPLOYEE			=C9/TotEmp	
11	AVERAGE COST PER HOUR				=D10/PHrs
12					
13	Tuition Reimbursement				
14	ANNUAL COST				
15	COST PER EMPLOYEE			=C14/TotEmp	
16	AVERAGE COST PER HOUR				=D15/PHrs
17					
18	Certification Lump Sum Payments				
19	ANNUAL COST				
20	COST PER EMPLOYEE			=C19/TotEmp	
21	AVERAGE COST PER HOUR				=D20/PHrs
22					
23	Education Differential Lump Sums				
24	ANNUAL COST				
25	COST PER EMPLOYEE			=C24/TotEmp	
26	AVERAGE COST PER HOUR				=D25/PHrs

The screen shot above shows five types of contractual 'annual benefits' and the formulas that are entered into the Format Worksheet. This worksheet could be compressed into one row for each type of benefit rather than the three rows used for purpose of illustration. From the ANNUAL COST received from the employer, COST PER EMPLOYEE and AVERAGE COST PER HOUR are calculated by dividing by total employees and productive hours.

The part of the Format Worksheet for pensions and SUB pay follows the same structure with the AVERAGE COST PER HOUR being expressed in column E. The formulas pre-entered for a defined-contribution pension plan, however, are different in that the contribution is often based on a flat hourly contribution, which can be entered in cell E41, from which TOTAL ANNUAL COST can be calculated. The comment in cell D40, however, suggests that the committee probably should not use PHrs here if pension contributions are made for all hours paid rather than just for productive hours.

	A	B	C	D	E	F
1	Format Worksheet #8 - Annual Payments & Allowances					
2						
3			Annual Cost	Cost Per Employee	Average Cost Per Hour	
34	Contribution to Defined Benefit Pension					
35	ANNUAL COST					
36	COST PER EMPLOYEE			=C35/TotEmp		
37	AVERAGE COST PER HOUR				=D36/PHrs	
38						
39	Contribution to 401 (k) Plan					
40	ANNUAL COST					
41	COST PER EMPLOYEE			=C40/TotEmp		
42	AVERAGE COST PER HOUR				=D41/PHrs	
43						
44	Contribution to Defined Contribution Pension					
45	ANNUAL COST			=D46*TotEmp		
46	COST PER EMPLOYEE				=E47*PHrs	
47	AVERAGE COST PER HOUR					
48						
49	Supplemental Unemployment Benefit Plan					
50	ANNUAL COST					
51	COST PER EMPLOYEE			=C50/TotEmp		
52	AVERAGE COST PER HOUR				=D51/PHrs	

This formula is the hourly contribution times PHrs. If pension contributions are made for hours paid (including holidays, vacation, etc.) you should use 2,080 hours

Data from the Regional Medical Center

The Regional Medical Center provided information that it reimbursed employees a total of $11,670 in the previous year for tuition fees. The AVERAGE COST PER HOUR is $0.07, as shown in the screen shot below. The collective agreement also provides that employees with more than 15 years of service are provided a longevity bonus of 1% of annual earnings; however, the medical center did not provide information on its annual cost.

The union committee can make an accurate estimate of the costs of longevity pay based on data it already has: the number of employees with more than 15 years of service, 8 full-time and 5 part-time employees, and an estimate of the average hourly/annual earnings of those 13 employees. The hourly earnings are calculated based on the average of the hourly wage rates for the five classifications at Step 15 (see cell G46 of the Data from the Employer worksheet). The formula used for the ANNUAL COST of the longevity bonus is 13 employees times .01 (1 percent) times the hourly average of the five Step 15 classifications times 2,080 hours. The AVERAGE COST PER HOUR for longevity pay is $0.03. Here it is assumed that the longevity payment is based on annual earnings, which include all paid hours. Therefore, 2,080 hours per year was used for that purpose.

The Regional Medical Center made a contribution to its defined-benefit plan of $224,053.68 in accordance with the amount calculated by the plan's actuary. The AVERAGE COST PER HOUR for the defined-benefit pension plan is $1.40 as shown in the screen shot below.

	A	B	C	D	E
1	RMC Worksheet #8 - Annual Payments & Allowances				
2					
3			Annual Cost	Cost Per Employee	Average Cost Per Hour
14	Tuition Reimbursement				
15	ANNUAL COST		$11,670.00		
16	COST PER EMPLOYEE			$121.56	
17	AVERAGE COST PER HOUR				$0.07
23					
24	Education Differential Lump Sums				
25	ANNUAL COST				
26	COST PER EMPLOYEE				
27	AVERAGE COST PER HOUR				
28					
29	Longevity Annual Payments				
30	ANNUAL COST		$5,406.55		
31	COST PER EMPLOYEE			$56.32	
32	AVERAGE COST PER HOUR				$0.03
33					
34	Contribution to Defined Benefit Pension				
35	ANNUAL COST		$224,053.68		
36	COST PER EMPLOYEE			$2,333.89	
37	AVERAGE COST PER HOUR				$1.40

This was calculated as 13 employees x .01 x 2080 hrs x an average of the five Step 15 rates (see cell G46 from data from the employer.

Chapter 10 – Summary of Contractual Costs and Roll-Up

AFTER CALCULATING the benefits/costs for contractual wages and most contractual benefits, the information can be pulled together into a concise summary sheet. Obviously, the most important data from each worksheet could be typed into a summary or be copied and pasted into a separate worksheet. But it makes more sense to create links between a summary page and the appropriate cells in the previous worksheets. By doing so, any changes that are made on an individual worksheet (due to new information or when preparing "what if" scenarios) would be automatically reflected on the summary page.

FORMAT WORKSHEET #9

	A	C	D	E
1	Format Worksheet #9 - Summary of Contractual Costs and Roll-Up Factor			
2				
3	Type of Fringe Benefit	TOTAL ANNUAL COST	ANNUAL COST PER EMPLOYEE	AVERAGE COST PER HOUR
4	Straight-Time (Base) Hourly Wage			='Ave Wage with Progression'!E45
5	**Daily/Weekly Overtime Premiums**			='Hourly Wage-Related Premiums'!E9
6	Flat Hourly Shift Differentials			='Hourly Wage-Related Premiums'!E17
7	**Percentage Hourly Shift Differentia**			='Hourly Wage-Related Premiums'!E24
8	Other Hourly Premiums			='Hourly Wage-Related Premiums'!E33
9	Skill-Based Premiums			='Hourly Wage-Related Premiums'!E42
10	**Paid Holidays Not Worked**			='Pay for Non-Work Time'!E8
11	**Personal Days**			='Pay for Non-Work Time'!E15
12	**Sick Leave**			='Pay for Non-Work Time'!E21
13	**Bereavement Leave**			='Pay for Non-Work Time'!E27
14	**Jury Duty Leave**			='Pay for Non-Work Time'!E33
15	**Leave for Union Business**			='Pay for Non-Work Time'!E39
16	Severance Pay			='Pay for Non-Work Time'!E44
17	**Vacations**			=Vacations!E12
18	Health Insurance			='Health & Life Insurance'!D19
19	Dental Insurance			='Health & Life Insurance'!D34
20	Life Insurance			='Health & Life Insurance'!F46
21	Disability/S&A Benefits			='Health & Life Insurance'!F52
22	Uniform Allowances			='Annual Payments&Allowances'!E7
23	Tool Alllowance/Replacement Costs			='Annual Payments&Allowances'!E12
24	Tuition Reimbursement			='Annual Payments&Allowances'!E17
25	Certification Lump Sums			='Annual Payments&Allowances'!E22
26	Education Differential Lump Sums			='Annual Payments&Allowances'!E27
27	**Longevity Annual Bonus/Payments**			='Annual Payments&Allowances'!E32
28	Defined Benefit Pension Contribution			='Annual Payments&Allowances'!E37
29	401 (k) Employer Contribution			='Annual Payments&Allowances'!E42
30	Defined Contribution Pension			='Annual Payments&Allowances'!E47
31	Supplemental Unemployment Benefits			='Annual Payments&Allowances'!E52
32	**TOTAL LABOR COST**			=SUM(E4:E31)
33				
34	Sum of Roll-Up Contractual Benefits			=E5+E7+E10+E11+E12+E13+E14+E15+E17+E27
35	**Roll-Up Factor**			=E34/E32

The screen shot above shows the links that have been pre-entered into Format Worksheet for the Summary of Contractual Benefits. The individual Format Worksheets generally have the AVERAGE COST PER HOUR for base wages and fringe benefits in column E. The summary worksheet is linked to the previous worksheets by selecting the appropriate cell in column E of the summary worksheet, for instance cell E4 for Straight-Time Average Hourly (Base) Wage, clicking it, entering = (as if starting a formula), then selecting either Worksheet #1 or Worksheet #2 and clicking the cell on that worksheet with the calculated Average Straight-Time Hourly Wage: cell E31 in Worksheet #1 or cell E45 in Worksheet #2. Or – if this cell has been named AveST – that name can be entered in cell E4. Each benefit listed on the summary worksheet can be linked to its appropriate AVERAGE COST PER HOUR from a previous worksheet.

Even if additional rows (or columns) are inserted into previous worksheets, or unneeded rows are deleted, Excel **should** adjust the linked cell designations to maintain the integrity of the summary worksheet. But this is only a 'should' and the user of any of these Format Worksheets **must** check that all links – as well as formulas – remain correct as a new workbook is being constructed for a particular bargaining unit.

Cell E32 is an AutoSum of the average wage and fringe benefits, including those that are blank and have no data linked from previous worksheets. Cell E32 is then an accurate estimate of the TOTAL (HOURLY) LABOR COST. Format Worksheet #9 is also designed for TOTAL ANNUAL COST to be captured in column C and ANNUAL COST PER EMPLOYEE to be captured in column D. These can be linked to the data in the previous worksheets or if the negotiating committee does not desire that much detail, just the totals can be calculated by multiplying by PHrs (productive hours) and TotEmp (total employees).

Roll-Up

Note in the screen shot that certain benefits are **bold**. These are benefits that are dependent on the level of the hourly wage. As wages increase the value of these benefits will increase. These are benefits that 'roll-up' as wage levels are increased. Other terms used for the same concept are 'add-on', 'creep', 'impact cost', and 'multiplying fringes'. Overtime premiums are a clear example of a benefit that rolls-up. Shift differentials based on a percentage of wages are another roll-up fringe, but 'flat' shift differentials are not. Most types of Pay for Non-Work Time (holidays, vacations, etc.) are generally based on an employee's hourly wage and therefore roll-up.

Some benefits can be indirectly connected to wage levels. For instance, severance pay that based on a certain number of weeks for each year of service at an employee's wage rate could be considered to be part of "roll-up" as could short-term disability (S&A benefits) that replace a certain percentage of employees' wages.

Should a defined benefit pension plan be included in roll-up? Though monthly pension benefits will likely have some relationship to employees' past earnings, it is often not a directly dependent relationship. An exception may be a pension plan that clearly defines an employee's monthly benefit to be 2% of average earnings per year of credited service. Even then, it is up to the actuary to make those calculations and to determine the annual payment to the pension plan. In this Format Worksheet, the cost of a defined-benefit pension plan has not been included in roll-up.

Format Worksheet #9 has a formula in cell E34 to sum the average costs of the roll-up benefits (the ones in bold). The 'roll-up factor' is cell E34 divided by the TOTAL HOURLY WAGE from cell E32 and is shown in cell E35. The roll-up factor can be easily interpreted. If wages increase by $1 per hour, other contractual benefits will roll-up by the percentage of the 'roll-up factor'. Note that cell E35 in the Format Worksheet has been pre-formatted to display as a percent.

	A	B	C	D	E
1	**RMC Worksheet #9 - Summary of Contractual Costs and Roll-Up Factor**				
2					
3	**Type of Fringe Benefit**		TOTAL ANNUAL COST	ANNUAL COST PER EMPLOYEE	AVERAGE COST PER HOUR
4	Straight-Time (Base) Hourly Wage				$17.07
5	**Daily/Weekly Overtime Premiums**				$0.29
6	Flat Hourly Shift Differentials				$0.78
7	**Percentage Hourly Shift Differentials**				
8	Other Hourly Premiums				
9	Skill-Based Premiums				
10	**Paid Holidays Not Worked**				$0.85
11	**Personal Days**				$0.21
12	**Sick Leave**				$0.39
13	**Bereavement Leave**				$0.02
14	Jury Duty Leave				
15	Leave for Union Business				
16	Severance Pay				
17	**Vacations**				$0.96
18	Health Insurance				$2.43
19	Dental Insurance				$0.73
20	Life Insurance				$0.18
21	Disability/S&A Benefits				
22	Uniform Allowances				
23	Tool Allowance/Replacement Costs				
24	Tuition Reimbursement				$0.07
25	Certification Lump Sums				
26	Education Differential Lump Sums				
27	**Longevity Annual Bonus/Payments**				$0.03
28	Defined Benefit Pension Contribution				$1.40
29	401 (k) Employer Contribution				
30	Defined Contribution Pension				
31	Supplemental Unemployment Benefits				
32	**TOTAL LABOR COST**		$4,076,762.75	$42,466.28	$25.41
33					
34	Sum of Roll-Up Contractual Benefits				$2.77
35	**Roll-Up Factor**				16.2%

RMC Summary and Roll-up Factor

The screen shot above shows the summary of the contractual costs at the Regional Medical Center. The average straight-time (base) wage is $17.07 and the total hourly labor cost is $25.41. The fringe benefits which roll-up are currently worth $2.77 per hour and the roll-up factor is 16.2%, meaning that a wage increase of $1.00 per hour would cost the employer $1.16. Note that the defined benefit pension plan has not been included in roll-up. If it was included the roll-up factor would be 24.4%.

The AVERAGE ANNUAL (LABOR) COST PER EMPLOYEE is $42,466 and the TOTAL ANNUAL (LABOR) COST is $4,076,763.

It is not necessary to try to entirely summarize the previous nine chapters and the worksheets they contain.

The intention has been to describe how to calculate the most accurate estimate of the average straight-time hourly wage at a particular point in time for bargaining units with and without step progression and to explore methods for calculating average wages for sub groups within a bargaining unit.

The most common benefits in collective agreements have been broadly categorized into Excel worksheet formats, according to the type of contractual benefit, and then their cost has been expressed in a consistent format: TOTAL ANNUAL COST, COST PER EMPLOYEE and AVERAGE COST PER HOUR.

These baseline costs are then linked to a one-page summary so that the union negotiating committee can see the overall structure of the wages and benefits that are in effect as it prepares to negotiate a new agreement.

Developing the worksheets also permits the union committee to double check certain information received from the employer for reasonableness and to determine whether to seek additional clarifying data.

Chapter 11 – Using the Workbook in Negotiations

FOR A UNION NEGOTIATING committee, the process of developing an Excel workbook similar to the Format Workbook is a valuable exercise in itself. But the real key is for the committee to use this information in:

- **planning for negotiations** by developing balanced, thoughtful and supportable proposals to take to the negotiating table, fully knowing their benefit to the members and the cost to the employer;
- **making good decisions at the negotiating table** by understanding the cost of the employer's proposals and the union's own counterproposals and knowing the impact of any potential trade-offs on the entire bargaining unit and subparts of it; and
- **reporting accurately to members during the ratification process** by explaining what was achieved and the overall value of the 'package'.

Having accurate baseline figures on wage rates for the bargaining unit (and any of its major subcategories: part-time, full-time, by classification, for 'skilled trades' and production workers, etc.) makes it much easier for the union negotiating committee to judge the impact of flat, across-the-board wage increases in comparison to percentage wage increases. If there is a step progression system, having the information in a worksheet makes it infinitely easier to make calculations of the effect of changing the increment between steps or the number of steps.

There are easy 'rules of thumb' that can be used after the baseline data is assembled. Knowing that in the RMC contract the 10 holidays cost the employer $.85 per hour makes it easy to estimate the cost of an additional holiday at around 8.5 cents per hour. Three personal days for full-time employees and two for part-time employees has the value of $.21 per hour. Doubling the number of days should cost the employer about the equivalent amount. Eliminating the personal days and transferring their value to wages could result in a wage increase of 21 cents per hour.

The level of detail and sophistication that any union negotiating committee desires is up to it and its 'costing expert'. Usually one member of the negotiating committee has the interest and has acquired the skills to fulfill this role. But it should not be his or her job alone. Every member of the committee, even if not preparing the worksheets or developing the formulas, must be aware of the methods and should be double checking all the figures for sense and sensibility.

The Medical Center Negotiations

Throughout the remainder of this chapter, the initial proposals of both the union and the Regional Medical Center will be added to the worksheets as well as several counterproposals and then the final agreement reached by the negotiators. For the sake of illustration, there is a fairly high level of detail. Obviously, estimates could be made in a simpler manner in some cases, like the 'rules of thumb' noted above.

However, once the baseline worksheets have been developed it is easy to add additional columns to the worksheets or copy and paste rows or 'blocks of cells' with the formulas previously prepared for the baseline year (2008 in the case of the RMC) which can then be used to calculate proposed or agreed-upon changes for future years.

Union Proposal #1

After surveying its members and analyzing their responses and examining comparable contracts in the industry and region and national trends in the health care industry and the current economic picture, the union has its initial proposal ready.

Its initial proposal is as follows for a two-year contract:
- Across-the-board general wage increases of 4.5% in the first year and 3.5% in the second;
- Increase the increment between wage steps from 1.8% to 2.0%;
- 1 additional holiday in 2009;
- Increase the number of personal days to 5 for full-time employees and 3 for part-time employees;
- 3 weeks of vacation for employees after 4 years of service (rather than 8 years);
- Reduce the insurance premium co-payment for all employees paying it, regardless of plan, by $30 per month;
- Increase longevity pay for those employees in Step 15 from 1% to 2%.

Cost estimates of the union's proposals are contained in a separate Excel workbook named Union Proposal #1 on the CD; it is based on the information in the RMC workbook, with projections for 2009 and 2010, developed in the manner described in this chapter. The first step to take is to save the RMC workbook (or your baseline workbook) with a new name, in this case, Union Proposal #1. This will leave the baseline calculations intact in that workbook and there is a 'mirror-image' of it in the newly-named workbook. The union committee can use the new 'proposal workbook' to enter changes that correspond with its proposal for 2009 and 2010.

Increment Increase and Percent Wage Increase

The first task is to project the benefits/costs of the proposed wage increases and the increase in the step increment. What is the negotiating committee's intention – to apply the general increase first and then to increase the increment? Does it make a difference? Most union negotiators will quickly answer that of course it makes a difference: apply the wage increase first and then increase the increments. So that is what is done to calculate the value of the union's proposals in the Average Wage with Progression worksheet.

First, additional columns must be designated for years 2009 and 2010. As shown in the following screen shot, this was done in columns F-H for 2009 and columns I-K for 2010. Columns B, D and E are hidden in this screen shot but remain in the actual worksheet, with column B listing the 15 steps, column D having the number of employees in each step and column E having the subtotals calculated as of 9/1/2008.

The wage rate for January 1, 2009 for the CM/CS Bachelors classification, Step 0 in cell F4 can be calculated as =C4*1.045 (a 4.5% increase). The subtotal will be =F4*G4. For January 1, 2010 the wage rate for this classification and step will be =F4*1.035 (a 3.5% increase) and the subtotal will be =I4*J4. These few pieces of information must be entered into the worksheet but nearly everything else, particularly the formulas, can be copied from the original columns. For instance, the subtotal formulas can be copied from cell E4 (not shown in the screen shot) and then pasted into H4 and K4.

	A	C	F	G	H	I	J	K
1	Union Proposal #1							
2			2009			2010		
3	Classification	Wage Rate as of 9/1/08	Wage Rate 1/1/09	# of Emp	Subtotal	Wage Rate 1/1/10	# of Emp	Subtotal
4	CM/CS Bachelors	15.5643	=C4*1.045	0	=F4*G4	=F4*1.035	0	=I4*J4
5	CM/CS Bachelors	=C4*1.018	=F4*1.02	2	=F5*G5	=I4*1.02	0	=I5*J5
6	CM/CS Bachelors	=C5*1.018	=F5*1.02	1	=F6*G6	=I5*1.02	2	=I6*J6
7	CM/CS Bachelors	=C6*1.018	=F6*1.02	2	=F7*G7	=I6*1.02	1	=I7*J7
8	CM/CS Bachelors	=C7*1.018	=F7*1.02	0	=F8*G8	=I7*1.02	2	=I8*J8
9	CM/CS Bachelors	=C8*1.018	=F8*1.02	3	=F9*G9	=I8*1.02	0	=I9*J9
10	CM/CS Bachelors	=C9*1.018	=F9*1.02	2	=F10*G10	=I9*1.02	3	=I10*J10
11	CM/CS Bachelors	=C10*1.018	=F10*1.02	3	=F11*G11	=I10*1.02	2	=I11*J11
12	CM/CS Bachelors	=C11*1.018	=F11*1.02	0	=F12*G12	=I11*1.02	3	=I12*J12
13	CM/CS Bachelors	=C12*1.018	=F12*1.02	5	=F13*G13	=I12*1.02	0	=I13*J13
14	CM/CS Bachelors	=C13*1.018	=F13*1.02	0	=F14*G14	=I13*1.02	5	=I14*J14
15	CM/CS Bachelors	=C14*1.018	=F14*1.02	4	=F15*G15	=I14*1.02	0	=I15*J15
16	CM/CS Bachelors	=C15*1.018	=F15*1.02	2	=F16*G16	=I15*1.02	4	=I16*J16
17	CM/CS Bachelors	=C16*1.018	=F16*1.02	0	=F17*G17	=I16*1.02	2	=I17*J17
18	CM/CS Bachelors	=C17*1.018	=F17*1.02	0	=F18*G18	=I17*1.02	0	=I18*J18
19	CM/CS Bachelors	=C18*1.018	=F18*1.02	10	=F19*G19	=I18*1.02	10	=I19*J19
20	TOTAL EEs and Total Hourly Wages fo			=SUM(G4:G19)	=SUM(H4:H19)		=SUM(J4:J19)	=SUM(K4:K19)
21	Average Hourly Rate for forCM/CS Ba				=H20/G20			=K20/J20
22	CM/CS Bachelors+23	16.48	=C22*1.045	0	=F22*G22	=F22*1.035	0	=I22*J22
23	CM/CS Bachelors+23	=C22*1.018	=F22*1.02	0	=F23*G23	=I22*1.02	0	=I23*J23
24	CM/CS Bachelors+23	=C23*1.018	=F23*1.02	1	=F24*G24	=I23*1.02	0	=I24*J24

Next, to increase the increment from 1.8% to 2.0% the only formula that must be entered is Cell F5 =F4*1.02. The remaining 13 progression steps in column F can be completed by using the AutoFill handle from cell F5. The same steps can be completed for column I or the formulas in column F can be copied and pasted into column I. Auto Sums can be inserted into row 20 or even niftier, the formulas in all four cells (D20, E20, D21 (empty) and E21) can be copied as a 'block' and pasted into G20 and J20 and Excel will make the appropriate column adjustments.

One other previous tip to keep in mind here is that after a cell formula is copied, it remains 'active' and ready to be pasted again until it is released by hitting the Esc key. For instance, once the formula in cell F4 is copied it can be pasted into the entire worksheet in the appropriate cells (in this case, in F22, F40, F58 and F76) for the four other job classifications. Then Esc can be executed to end the copying/pasting function.

How many employees are in each wage step? The union committee could decide to leave the distribution 'frozen' as it was on 9/1/2008. Instead, this worksheet assumes that no new employees will be hired and that every member will move up one additional progression step during the course of the year. To calculate the new distribution enter zero employees in Step 0 for 2009, copy the entire distribution of employees as of 9/1/2008, and paste it into cell G5 and then add together the number of employees now in Step 15 (6 before, plus 4 additional employees = 10).

	A	B	D	F	G	I	J
1	Union Proposal #1 - Step Advancement						
2				2009		2010	
3	Classification	Step	Number of Employees	Wage Rate 1/1/09	# of Emp	Wage Rate 1/1/10	# of Emp
4	CM/CS Bachelors	0	2	=C4*1.045	0	=F4*1.035	0
5	CM/CS Bachelors	1	1	=F4*1.02	2	=I4*1.02	0
6	CM/CS Bachelors	2	2	=F5*1.02	1	=I5*1.02	=G5
7	CM/CS Bachelors	3	0	=F6*1.02	2	=I6*1.02	=G6
8	CM/CS Bachelors	4	3	=F7*1.02	0	=I7*1.02	=G7
9	CM/CS Bachelors	5	2	=F8*1.02	3	=I8*1.02	=G8
10	CM/CS Bachelors	6	3	=F9*1.02	2	=I9*1.02	=G9
11	CM/CS Bachelors	7	0	=F10*1.02	3	=I10*1.02	=G10
12	CM/CS Bachelors	8	5	=F11*1.02	0	=I11*1.02	=G11
13	CM/CS Bachelors	9	0	=F12*1.02	5	=I12*1.02	=G12
14	CM/CS Bachelors	10	4	=F13*1.02	0	=I13*1.02	=G13
15	CM/CS Bachelors	11	2	=F14*1.02	4	=I14*1.02	=G14
16	CM/CS Bachelors	12	0	=F15*1.02	2	=I15*1.02	=G15
17	CM/CS Bachelors	13	0	=F16*1.02	0	=I16*1.02	=G16
18	CM/CS Bachelors	14	4	=F17*1.02	0	=I17*1.02	=G17
19	CM/CS Bachelors	15	6	=F18*1.02	10	=I18*1.02	=G18+G19
20	TOTAL EEs and Total Hourly Wages forCM		=SUM(D4:D19)		=SUM(G4:G19)		=SUM(J4:J19)
21	Average Hourly Rate for forCM/CS Bachel						

An alternate approach is shown for the year 2010. The number of employees in Step 2 (cell J6) is the number that was previously in Step 1 (cell G5) and the number of employees in Step 15 in 2010 is the sum of those in Steps 14 and 15 in 2009. This is a level of precision that may not be necessary for the union (though the employer might certainly point out this 'seniority creep'). It will tend to at least slightly overstate the cost to the employer as it is likely that some senior employees will leave over the course of the new contract and new employees would presumably start at wage step 0.

After the formulas are inserted for all classifications for both years, summary statistics can be calculated for 2009 and 2010. Again, it is possible to copy the formulas used in columns D and E and paste them into columns G/H and columns J/K, with some caution. If you copy the formulas in E101 and E102 which were based on the number of hours for full-time and part-time employees from the Productive Hours worksheet, Excel will be 'too smart' and change the cell designations from that worksheet to cells that are empty). Check the formulas and watch out for numbers that do not look right!

	A	E	G	H	J	K
1	Union Proposal #1 - Wage and Increment Increase					
2		2008		2009		2010
94						
95	TOTAL # of Employees and Total Hourly Wages	$1,638.61	96	$1,771.16	96	$1,860.75
96	Average Straight-Time Hourly Wage:	$17.07		$18.45		$19.38
97						
98	Average ST Hourly Rate for F-T CM/CS Classification:	$18.72		$20.23		$21.23
99	Average ST Hourly Rate for P-T RN Classification:	$15.11		$16.35		$17.20
100						
101	Annual Payroll for F-T CM/CS Classification:	$2,032,791.71		$2,196,274.23		$2,305,045.06
102	Annual Payroll for P-T RN Classification:	$1,041,465.92		$1,126,426.71		$1,185,151.11
103	TOTAL Annual ST Payroll based on Scheduled Hours	$3,074,257.63		$3,322,700.94		$3,490,196.17

The screen shot above, with many rows and columns hidden, shows the overall cost of the union's proposals for a general wage increase of 4.5% and an increase in the increment from 1.8% to 2.0% in the first year and a general wage increase of 3.5% in the second year. The Average Straight-Time Hourly Wage would increase from $17.07 to $18.45 (an increase of just less than 8.1%) in the first year and to $19.38 in the second year (an increase of just over 5.0%).

There is also a breakdown for full-time and part-time employees (part-time employees, on average, have a slightly greater percentage increase). The Regional Medical Center's annual payroll based on scheduled hours increases from $3.074 million to $3.490 million over the two years. Cell H96 has also been named 'AveST09' and cell K96 has been named 'AveST10'. And cells H98 and K98 have been named AveFT09 and AveFT10, respectively while cells H99 and K99 have been named AvePT09 and AvePT10.

Excel Basics – Adjusting column margins
If the reader has been following the steps in this manual and in the actual worksheets and has been toggling back and forth (Ctrl ~) between the formulas and the actual values, you have likely been frustrated by the fact that Excel does not keep the column widths as they were originally set. It is possible to "auto fit" the size of the columns to the data (or formulas) in them by selecting the columns you want to adjust, clicking Cells and Format on the tool bar and selecting Auto Fit Column Width from the drop down menu. Or you might find it easier to adjust columns 'by hand' at the top of the worksheet by 'dragging the margin markers' as it permits a tighter fit of the data, albeit with a bit more work.

Holidays and Personal Days

The union is proposing one additional holiday for all employees for a total of 11 per year and two additional personal days for full-time employees (total 5) and one additional personal day for part-time employees (total 3). The following screen shot shows the cost for the additional holiday for 2009 and 2010. The reader is referred to the actual worksheet for the formulas but essentially it is now 11 holidays*8 hours*the rate paid for each holiday to calculate the COST PER EMPLOYEE. The rate paid for holidays in 2009 is AveST09, from the above worksheet, plus the AveSD (the average shift differential, which should be the same flat amount as in 2008 since the union is not proposing any change).

	A	E	F	G	H	I	J	K
1	Union Proposal #1							
2								
3	Holidays			2009			2010	
4	Number of Paid Holidays	AVERAGE COST PER HOUR 2008	Rate Paid for Each Holiday	COST PER EMPLOYEE	AVE COST PER HOUR	Rate Paid for Each Holiday	COST PER EMPLOYEE	AVE COST PER HOUR
5	10		$19.23	$1,691.85		$20.16	$1,773.98	
6	Holiday Hours Paid/Not Worked:		8448			8448		
7	ANNUAL COST		$162,417.85			$170,302.02		
8	AVERAGE COST PER HOUR	$0.85			$1.01			$1.06
9								
10	Personal Days							
11	Number of Paid Personal Days	AVERAGE COST PER HOUR	Rate Paid for Each Leave Day	COST PER EMPLOYEE	AVERAGE COST PER HOUR	Rate Paid for Each Leave Day	COST PER EMPLOYEE	AVERAGE COST PER HOUR
12	3 for F-T Employees		$20.23	$809.12		$21.23	$849.19	
13	2 for P-T Employees		$16.35	$392.35		$17.20	$412.80	
14	Annual Personal Hours Paid		2080			2080		
15	ANNUAL COST		$59,337.46			$62,321.19		
16	AVERAGE COST PER HOUR	$0.21			$0.37			$0.39

The AVERAGE COST PER HOUR is based on the COST PER EMPLOYEE divided by Productive Hours. The observant reader (and probably the employer) will note that the number of productive hours in 2009 and in 2010 will be less than in 2008 because of the additional holiday, vacations and the additional hours of paid personal leave that the union is proposing. However, since these proposals have not been agreed to, the same number of productive hours calculated for 2008 are used in this worksheet for 2009 and 2010. If the changes proposed by the union are agreed upon, the calculation of productive hours can be adjusted accordingly and can be named as PHrs09 and PHrs10.

As shown, the 11th holiday would cost the Regional Medical Center an additional $.16 in 2009. So the rule of thumb that one holiday would cost around 8.5 cents per hour does not hold very well when the union's proposed wage and increment increases are incorporated into the calculation. The cost of the 11th holiday in 2010 is an additional 5 cents, entirely due to roll-up from the proposed second year increase in wages. The reader is encouraged to look at the formulas in the actual worksheet. They are not shown here in the manual.

The calculation of the cost to the employer of the additional paid personal days mirrors the formulas of the original 2008 calculation except now the rate paid for the five leave days for full-time employees is set equal to the 2009 average wage of (AveFT09) and the rate for the three days for part-time employees is set equal to AvePT09. It is also updated for year 2010. In 2009, the union's proposal would increase the AVERAGE COST PER HOUR of personal days from $.21 to $.37, with an additional increase in cost in 2010 to $.39 due entirely to the proposed wage increase in 2010.

Vacations

	A	B	C	G	H	I	J	K
1	Union Proposal #1, Vacation Eligibility							
65	Vacation Eligibility Schedule				Years of Service	# of Weeks		
66					<4 years	2		
67					>4<15 years	3		
68					>15<25	4		
69					>25	5		
70	Part-time employees shall receive a pro-rata benefit for v:							
71								
72	Seniority Schedule	2008		2009			Vacation Eligibilty	
73	Years of Service	Full-Time	Part-Time	Full-Time	Part-Time	Total	Full-Time	Part-Time
74	0<1	1	1	0	0	=G74+H74		
75	1<2	1	4	=B74	=C74	=G75+H75		
76	2<3	1	3	=B75	=C75	=G76+H76		
77	3<4	5	2	=B76	=C76	=G77+H77	=SUM(G74:G77)	=SUM(H74:H77)
78	4<5	1	1	=B77	=C77	=G78+H78		
79	5<6	0	3	=B78	=C78	=G79+H79		
80	6<7	7	4	=B79	=C79	=G80+H80		
81	7<8	9	3	=B80	=C80	=G81+H81		
82	8<9	5	0	=B81	=C81	=G82+H82		
83	9<10	2	4	=B82	=C82	=G83+H83		
84	10<11	3	3	=B83	=C83	=G84+H84		
85	11<12	3	3	=B84	=C84	=G85+H85		
86	12<13	3	3	=B85	=C85	=G86+H86		
87	13<14	2	3	=B86	=C86	=G87+H87		
88	14<15	1	2	=B87	=C87	=G88+H88	=SUM(G78:G88)	=SUM(H78:H88)
89	15<16	0	0	=B88	=C88	=G89+H89		

The union's proposal adds a third week of vacation after four years of service. The screen shot above, with some rows and columns hidden, shows how the seniority schedule in Worksheet #10 – Data from the Employer can be modified to determine how many employees would be eligible for the third week of vacation in 2009. It also includes the movement of all employees to have one additional year of service in 2009, the so-called 'seniority creep'.

A formula is used to determine how many employees have moved into the additional year of seniority in 2009 in columns G and H. G74 and H74 are entered as zero (no new hires) and those with 1<2 years of service in 2009 are those who had 0<1 years of service in 2008 (G75=B74, etc.).

Chapter 11 – Using the Workbook in Negotiations

Once the first formulas are entered in G75 and H75, the rest of the column can be completed with the Auto Fill handle except for the last row (not shown) which must be the sum of the employees with 24 and >25 years of service in 2008.

Because part-time employees have pro-rata vacation and the union has not proposed any change, the worksheet again captures how many full-time and part-time employees are in each vacation eligibility category. The full-time employees eligible for two weeks vacation are the sum of G74:G77 and the part-time H74:77. The employees eligible for the third week of vacation are summed in row 88. The number of employees in each vacation category can then be linked to the vacation worksheet.

	A	E	F	G	H	I	J
19	**Union Proposal #1 -Vacation Pay**						
20		2008		2009			
21	Number of Days or Weeks of Vacation for Each Category	SUBTOTAL COST	Number of Days or Weeks of Vacation for	Number of Hours Paid	Number of Eligible Employees	Vacation Pay Rate	SUBTOTAL COST
22	Full-time employees		Full-time employees				
23	2		2	80	3		
24	3		3	120	40		
25	4		4	160	7		
26	5		5	200	2		
27	Subtotal	$104,095.95	Subtotal		6560	$20.23	$132,695.61
28	Part-time employees		Part-time employees				
29	2		2	60	8		
30	3		3	90	29		
31	4		4	120	7		
32	5		5	150	0		
33	Subtotal	$52,599.29	Subtotal		3930	$16.35	$64,246.73
34	Total Hours of Paid Vacation:		Total Hours of Paid Vacation:		10490		
35	ANNUAL COST		ANNUAL COST			$196,942.35	
36	ANNUAL COST PER E	$1,632.24	ANNUAL COST PER EMPLOYEE				$2,051.48
37	AVERAGE COST PER	$0.98	AVERAGE COST PER HOUR				$1.23

RMC Worksheet #6a is used for the calculation of costs for 2009. Here the entire block of cells used for the 2008 calculation (A21 to E21 down to A37 to E37) is highlighted and copied and then pasted into cell F21. There is now a mirror image of the format and formulas and only the number of employees eligible for each vacation category and the vacation pay rate for 2009 need to be entered. The number of eligible employees (based on the union's proposal and 'seniority creep') is linked from the Data from the Employer worksheet. The vacation pay rate for full-time employees is entered as =AveFT09 and the rate for part-time employees is =AvePT09.

The union's vacation proposal will increase the Average Cost per Hour from $.98 to $1.23 in 2009.

A similar process can be followed if the union wishes to project the costs for 2010 by again copying and pasting the block of cells with the formulas, typing in headings for that year and then using AveFT10 and AvePT10 for the rate at which holidays are paid. Be careful in case Excel is 'too smart' and has pasted different cells for the number of eligible employees. Though there will 'seniority creep' in 2010 and vacation eligibility will change slightly, it is probably not worth capturing in the worksheet.

> **Excel Basics – Copying and pasting *values***
> Another important feature of Excel permits pasting the *value* of cells rather than the entire contents (i.e. the formulas or links to previous worksheet cells). In this case the number of employees eligible for vacation in 2009 are copied, then Paste Special is selected, and from the drop down menu, paste *Values* is chosen. In this way only the values from cells H23 to H26 (the actual number of full-time employees) and from H29 to H32 (the number of part-time employees) will be pasted into column M for 2010, rather than the (incorrect) links back to the Data from the Employer worksheet.

Health Insurance

The union's initial proposal is to reduce insurance premium co-payments by $30 per month for both the indemnity plan and the HMO plan. To calculate the additional cost to the employer (and the reduced cost to those employees who are currently making co-payments) a block of cells from C3 to F3, down to C31 and F31 is copied and pasted into cell G3. Because the employer's premium cost was set up in the original spreadsheet to be the total monthly premium less the employees' share, only the employee amount in column G needs to be reduced by $30.

Because an *incomplete* 'mirror image' (it did not include the column with the number of covered employees) was copied and pasted, Excel misinterprets many of the formulas for 2009. But they can be quickly reconstructed and validated. As shown in the screen shot, the employer's annual cost for health insurance increases by about $22,000 and its Average Cost per Hour increases from $2.43 to $2.57. The average employee contribution per hour for the 63 employees contributing drops from $.63 to $.41. Note that this calculation does not include any overall cost increase for health insurance in 2009. That will be discussed later after the union receives the first proposal from the Regional Medical Center.

	A	B	C	D	G	H	I	J
1	Union Proposal #1 - Health Insurance							
2			2008		2009			
3	Type of Health Coverage	Number of Enrolled	Employee's Monthly Premium	Employer's Monthly Premium	Employee's Monthly Premium	Employer's Monthly Premium	TOTAL Monthly Premium	TOTAL ANNUAL COST
4	Indemnity Plan							
5	Single Employee	10	$0.00	$327.40	$0.00	$327.40	$327.40	$39,288.00
6	Family	6	$90.00	$720.62	$60.00	$750.62	$810.62	$58,364.64
7	Single + 1 Dependent	4	$60.00	$542.90	$30.00	$572.90	$602.90	$28,939.20
8	P-T Single Employee	6	$90.00	$237.40	$60.00	$267.40	$327.40	$23,572.80
9	P-T Family	2	$180.00	$630.62	$150.00	$660.62	$810.62	$19,454.88
10	P-T Single + 1 Dependent	3	$120.00	$482.90	$90.00	$512.90	$602.90	$21,704.40
15	HMO Plan							
16	Single Employee	8	$0.00	$247.74	$0.00	$247.74	$247.74	$23,783.04
17	Family	12	$70.00	$491.62	$40.00	$521.62	$561.62	$80,873.28
18	Single + 1 Dependent	12	$50.00	$376.68	$20.00	$406.68	$426.68	$61,441.92
19	P-T Single Employee	3	$70.00	$177.74	$40.00	$207.74	$247.74	$8,918.64
20	P-T Family	8	$140.00	$421.62	$110.00	$451.62	$561.62	$53,915.52
21	P-T Single + 1 Dependent	7	$100.00	$326.68	$70.00	$356.68	$426.68	$35,841.12
22	EMPLOYER'S TOTAL MONTHLY COST			$32,498.12		$34,388.12		
23	EMPLOYER'S ANNUAL COST			$389,977.44		$412,657.44		
24	ANNUAL COST PER EMPLOYEE			$4,062.27		$4,298.52		
25	AVERAGE COST PER HOUR			$2.43		$2.57		
26	Enrolled employees	81						
27	Employees' Total Monthly Contributions		$5,510.00		$3,620.00			
28	Employees' Annual Contributions		$66,120.00		$43,440.00			
29	Average Cost Per Employee Contributing		$1,049.52		$689.52			
30	Average Employee Contribution Per Hour		$0.63		$0.41			
31	Total Cost for Health Insurance						$456,097.44	$456,097.44

Longevity Annual Bonus

The union's proposes to increase the longevity bonus for employees with >15 years of service from 1% to 2% of annual earnings. Simple logic would indicate that the employer's cost should double. But sometimes such logic is not totally accurate. A careful look at the number of employees in the step progression would show that in 2009 21 employees would be in Step 15 assuming that progression into the next step is automatic. And eligible employees' annual earnings would be based on the union's wage proposal for 2009. On this basis, the employer's Average Cost per Hour for longevity in 2009 would increase from $.04 to $.12 if the union's proposal is accepted.

The actual formula in cell F30 (not shown in the screen shot) is created entirely with links to other parts of the workbook. If it is reviewed in the formula bar of the worksheet it may look complicated, but if the reader traces it back to its original worksheets it is quite straightforward.

	A	B	C	D	E	F	G	H
1	**Union Proposal #1 - Longevity**							
2				2008			2009	
29	Longevity Annual Payments							
30	ANNUAL COST		$5,822.44			$18,798.73		
31	COST PER EMPLOYEE			$60.65			$195.82	
32	AVERAGE COST PER HOUR				$0.04			$0.12
33								
38								
53								
54								
55								
56								
57								
58								
59								

Callout on C30/D31: This was calculated as 14 employees x .01 x 2080 hrs x an average of the five Step 15 rates (see cell G46 from data from the employer.

Callout on F30/G31/H32: This was calculated as 21 employees x .02 x 2080 hrs x an average of the five Step 15 rates for 2009. Though this formula looks complicated, it shows very well how cells in worksheets can be linked.

Summary of Union Proposal #1

The union negotiating committee will certainly want to see an overall picture of the benefits/costs of the proposals it will take to the bargaining table. It is easy to link the information calculated in the individual worksheets to the summary worksheet. Columns must be designated for 2009 and 2010. Then the data is linked to this page, as previously described. The screen shot shows the impact of the union's proposal for both 2009 and 2010. Some columns are hidden as well as the rows with benefits that are not part of the Regional Medical Center contract. Note that costs are calculated for those benefits that roll up for 2009 and 2010 even though the union proposed no changes in their terms.

For those fringe benefits for which the union has not proposed any change in 2009 and which do not roll up, for instance shift differentials, the cost for 2009 is set equal to 2008, that is F6=E6 and for 2010, G6=F6. These can be modified later in the summary page if some further change is proposed by either party during the course of negotiations. Updated roll-up factors are calculated for 2009 and 2010 – the additional holiday, vacation and personal leave days have a visible effect on the roll-up factor.

A new part in this summary worksheet is the last row in which a percentage increase for each year is calculated. Though the formula is not shown on the screen shot, for cell F36 for 2009 it is =F31-E31/E31. Once this formula is entered it can be copied and pasted into cell G36 to calculate the percent increase in 2010.

The union's proposal for 2009, including roll-up costs, will represent an 8.82% increase in hourly costs. Its proposals for 2010 would increase costs by 4.08%.

Contract Costing for Union Negotiators

	A	E	F	G	H
1	**Union Proposal #1 - Summary of Costs**				
2					
3	Type of Fringe Benefit	AVERAGE COST PER HOUR 2008	2009	2010	2011
4	Straight-Time (Base) Hourly Wage	$17.07	$18.45	$19.38	
5	Daily/Weekly Overtime Premiums	$0.29	$0.32	$0.33	
6	Flat Hourly Shift Differentials	$0.78	$0.78	$0.78	
10	Paid Holidays Not Worked	$0.85	$1.01	$1.06	
11	Personal Days	$0.21	$0.37	$0.39	
12	Sick Leave	$0.39	$0.42	$0.44	
13	Bereavement Leave	$0.02	$0.02	$0.02	
17	Vacations	$0.96	$1.23	$1.29	
18	Health Insurance	$2.43	$2.57	$2.57	
19	Dental Insurance	$0.73	$0.73	$0.73	
20	Life Insurance	$0.18	$0.18	$0.18	
23	Tuition Reimbursement	$0.07	$0.07	$0.07	
26	Longevity Annual Payments	$0.04	$0.12	$0.14	
27	Defined Benefit Pension Contribution	$1.40	$1.40	$1.40	
31	TOTAL LABOR COST	$25.42	$27.66	$28.79	
32					
33	Sum of Roll-Up Contractual Benefits	$2.77	$3.49	$3.68	
34	Roll-Up Factor	16.2%	18.9%	19.0%	
35					
36	Percent Increase Each Year		8.82%	4.08%	

Regional Medical Center Proposal #1

After several negotiating sessions mostly dedicated to the union explaining its proposal and its rationale, the union committee requested that the employer put a proposal on the table. At the negotiating session early that week, the employer laid out this proposal:

- A three year agreement;
- Maintenance of the two existing health care plans without changes but with the employees paying all the *projected* increases in premium costs: indemnity plan – increases of 10% in 2009, 8% in 2010 and 5% in 2011 and the HMO plan – a 6% increase each year;
- It is open to the idea of increasing the step increment in order to retain long-service employees or increasing the longevity annual payment but not both – and the increment increase should be implemented before any general wage increase;
- Reduce shift differentials to 6% of an employee's hourly wage on second shift and to 10% of an employee's hourly wage on third shift;
- It will consider a modest improvement in the vacation schedule so that employees with 6 or more years of service will receive a third week of vacation.
- A general wage increase of $.40 in 2009; $.30 in 2010; and $.30 in 2011.

Chapter 11 – Using the Workbook in Negotiations

The union responded that the employer's proposal is certainly not acceptable to members of the bargaining unit but that it will carefully review the proposal and respond at the next bargaining session.

Flat Wage Increase and Increment Increase

The easiest way to cost the employer's proposal is to use the format of Union Proposal #1 workbook (since future years and some formulas have been added already) and to make a separate workbook for the employer's proposal. Union Proposal #1 workbook is saved with a new name, RMC Proposal #1, and work can start in modifying the wage and progression worksheet to conform to the employer's proposal.

Because the employer said it would agree to an increment increase applied before any wage increase, that is the first step. The Step 0 wage rate for the first classification in cell F4 is set equal to the 2008 rate. Cell F4's formula can be copied and pasted into C22 and Step 0 of the other classifications. The Step 1 progression is increased from 1.8% to 2.0% (the same as the union's proposal) with the formula F5 =F4*1.02 and steps 2 to 15 are completed using the Auto Fill handle in cell F5. The same procedure is followed for all five classifications. Since the union had already entered the number of employees in each step, including 'seniority creep', that part is done.

To add in the $.40 wage increase a column is inserted by highlighting column G, right clicking and choosing insert from the drop down menu. There is now a column which can be labeled "Flat wage increase of $.40". The wage rate in cell G4 is simply =F4+.40. This formula can then be auto filled or copied for all the other steps in all the classifications for 2009. The wage rates for 2010 are the previous year's rate (in column G) plus $.30. Three additional columns are designated for 2011, with another $.30 added to the rates. For the number of employees in each step in 2011 it really is not necessary to account for 'seniority creep' two years hence as surely there would be retirements and other changes by that time. The distribution of employees in steps in 2010 is just copied and pasted into year 2011.

Finally, the formulas for classification and employee subtotals and the average wage for each classification can be copied as a block (K20 to L20, down one row to K21 and L21) and the block can be pasted in cells N20, N38, N56, N74 and N92. As shown in the screen shot below, for just the classification of CM/CS Bachelors classification, the employer's wage proposal has been rather quickly calculated for further analysis by the union negotiating committee.

RMC Proposal #1 - Wage and Increment Increase

Classification	Step	Increment Wage Rate 1/1/09	Flat wage increase of $.40	# of Emp	Subtotal	Wage Rate 1/1/10	# of Emp	Subtotal	Wage Rate 1/1/11	# of Emp	Subtotal
CM/CS Bachelors	0	$15.5643	$15.9643	0	$0.00	$16.2643	0	$0.00	$16.5643	0	$0.00
CM/CS Bachelors	1	$15.8756	$16.2756	2	$32.55	$16.5756	0	$0.00	$16.8756	0	$0.00
CM/CS Bachelors	2	$16.1931	$16.5931	1	$16.59	$16.8931	2	$33.79	$17.1931	2	$34.39
CM/CS Bachelors	3	$16.5170	$16.9170	2	$33.83	$17.2170	1	$17.22	$17.5170	1	$17.52
CM/CS Bachelors	4	$16.8473	$17.2473	0	$0.00	$17.5473	2	$35.09	$17.8473	2	$35.69
CM/CS Bachelors	5	$17.1842	$17.5842	3	$52.75	$17.8842	0	$0.00	$18.1842	0	$0.00
CM/CS Bachelors	6	$17.5279	$17.9279	2	$35.86	$18.2279	3	$54.68	$18.5279	3	$55.58
CM/CS Bachelors	7	$17.8785	$18.2785	3	$54.84	$18.5785	2	$37.16	$18.8785	2	$37.76
CM/CS Bachelors	8	$18.2361	$18.6361	0	$0.00	$18.9361	3	$56.81	$19.2361	3	$57.71
CM/CS Bachelors	9	$18.6008	$19.0008	5	$95.00	$19.3008	0	$0.00	$19.6008	0	$0.00
CM/CS Bachelors	10	$18.9728	$19.3728	0	$0.00	$19.6728	5	$98.36	$19.9728	5	$99.86
CM/CS Bachelors	11	$19.3523	$19.7523	4	$79.01	$20.0523	0	$0.00	$20.3523	0	$0.00
CM/CS Bachelors	12	$19.7393	$20.1393	2	$40.28	$20.4393	4	$81.76	$20.7393	4	$82.96
CM/CS Bachelors	13	$20.1341	$20.5341	0	$0.00	$20.8341	2	$41.67	$21.1341	2	$42.27
CM/CS Bachelors	14	$20.5368	$20.9368	0	$0.00	$21.2368	0	$0.00	$21.5368	0	$0.00
CM/CS Bachelors	15	$20.9475	$21.3475	10	$213.47	$21.6475	10	$216.47	$21.9475	10	$219.47
TOTAL EEs and Total Hourly Wages for CM/CS Ba				34	$654.19		34	$673.01		34	$683.21
Average Hourly Rate for forCM/CS Bachelors					$19.24			$19.79			$20.09

To see the overall average wage rates for each year and the breakdown for full-time and part-time employees as well as the annual payroll, copy the whole block (K95 to L95 down one row to K96, L96), previously done in Union Proposal #1 and paste it into cell N95 and follow the same procedure for the full-time and part-time averages. The bottom of the worksheet now looks like the following screen shot.

RMC Proposal #1 - Wage and Increment Increase

		Increment Wage Rate 1/1/09	Flat wage increase of $.40	# of Emp	Subtotal	Wage Rate 1/1/10	# of Emp	Subtotal	Wage Rate 1/1/11	# of Emp	Subtotal
Classification	Step										
TOTAL # of Employees and Total Hourly Wages				96	$1,733.29		96	$1,787.61		96	$1,816.41
Average Straight-Time Hourly Wage:					$18.06			$18.62			$18.92
Average ST Hourly Rate for F-T CM/CS Classification:					$19.76			$20.33			$20.63
Average ST Hourly Rate for P-T RN Classification:					$16.04			$16.60			$16.90
Annual Payroll for F-T CM/CS Classification:					$2,145,128			$2,207,196			$2,239,769
Annual Payroll for P-T RN Classification:					$1,105,482			$1,143,997			$1,164,668
TOTAL Annual ST Payroll based on Scheduled Hours					$3,250,610			$3,351,193			$3,404,437

The average straight-time hourly wage for 2009 (after the increment increase, the $.40 general increase and seniority creep) has risen from $17.07 to $18.06. Even more striking is that the average straight-time hourly wage for 2010 has increased to

$18.62 based on the $.30 general wage increase and a significant impact from seniority creep. Since the union did not adjust for any seniority creep in 2011, the average increased by just the 30 cent general increase. Seniority creep, coupled with an increase in the increment between wage steps, can have a powerful impact on employees' earnings and the employer's costs.

Excel Basics – Formatting pages for printing
Because the union committee would certainly like to make a detailed comparison of both the union's wage proposal and the employer's wage proposal, this is probably a good time to briefly review some of the options for further formatting and printing of worksheets. Obviously, too big or too small printouts make it difficult to understand or compare proposals. The first item to consider is which rows or columns can be hidden without losing valuable information. Then, does what remains fit on one standard page? In Excel you can request print previews as in MS Word; you can also adjust printing margins as wide or long as your printer will permit; you can try changing the print output from portrait to landscape; or you can also 'order' Excel to print the output on just one page – but you may not be very happy with the readability of what you get.

Print titles
Once you have made as many adjustments as you can it still might be that all the important rows do not fit on one page or some of the columns continue onto a second page. This is annoying, particularly if it is important to see the row or column headings. Fortunately, Excel has a function in which row or column headings can be repeated on the second and subsequent pages. The instruction is a little tricky but manageable. Most of the key instructions are found in Page Setup. Here you can change the page size, margins, orientation, set a specific print area, add page breaks or request that titles be repeated on subsequent pages. You can 'click in' the row or column titles you want repeated and it will appear in the 'Print titles' boxes or the instruction can be typed in. To repeat row 1, for instance, the instruction in the box will look like $1:$1 and to repeat column A, it will be $A:$A.

Print gridlines and headings
Another consideration is whether to print gridlines and the column and row headings (i.e. column A, B, etc. and row numbers). Gridlines are usually very helpful to a reader; the column and row headings are optional but if you want to refer someone specifically to cell J25, then the column and row headings are indispensable.

Borders
Judiciously adding borders to the worksheet will make it more readable and understandable. Separating years with a border certainly makes sense. The selection of possible borders is extensive as is the ability to change font and size, to highlight, to color cells, and so forth. Just don't overdo it – the goal is a readable worksheet, not a work of art.

Health Insurance

The employer proposed that the employees pay the additional cost of health insurance premiums over the course of a three-year agreement. Though it is the kind of proposal to which the union might give a short and emphatic 'no' it also makes some sense to calculate the actual impact on employees so that it can be used both at the bargaining table and as a tool in mobilizing employees against the proposal.

Unfortunately in this case, the union formatted its health insurance worksheet so that the employer's premium cost was the total premium less the employees' share. The employer's proposal asks that *its* costs be frozen for three years. So some modifications to the Union Proposal #1 worksheet must be made. This is an opportunity to illustrate a few other features of Excel.

Since the employer's premium for 2008 and 2009 in both columns D and G is based on the total premium less the employee's share, it is necessary to find a way to modify this formula. The employer's premiums for 2008 for each group could be manually entered into each row in column H or cells D5 to D10 (for the indemnity plan) and cells D16 to D21 (for the HMO plan) can be copied and then pasted into column H as *values* using the Paste Special instruction and Paste Values selection from the drop down menu. This way these values are now fixed and the employees' premiums can be calculated as the total monthly premium minus the employer's (fixed) share.

Recalling that there were problems in the union proposal worksheet in *retaining the correct formulas* because the number of employees in each category (column B) was not copied over to 2009, you might decide to make the 'block of columns' symmetrical for 2009, 2010 and 2011. A new column is inserted for 2009, column G, and the data from column B (the number of employees in each plan) is copied and pasted into the new column. Now there is a 'block' for 2009 that is symmetrical to 2008 and the formulas should be ok.

The total monthly premiums for 2009 in each category can now be increased by 10% for the indemnity plan and 6% for the HMO plan in column I by using the formula I5=E5*1.10 (a 10% increase) and then filled down the next five rows; cell I16 has the formula =E16*1.06 (a 6% increase) and then is filled down. Since *all* of the other formulas remain intact, the union committee can quickly see that the employees' premiums increase from just over $66,000 to over $101,000. Since all employees are now contributing, based on the employer's proposal, the average cost per employee is $1,248 per year and the cost per hour is $.75, using 81 enrolled employees as the divisor.

The entire block for 2009 (G2 to K2, down to G31 to K31) is then copied and pasted into cells L2 and Q2. Now there are formats and formulas to calculate the costs for 2010 and 2011. The total premium for the indemnity plan increases by 8% in 2010 and 5% in 2011; and the HMO plan increases by 6% in both years. These formulas must be entered once but then they can be copied down using the fill handle and the remaining calculations of employer and employee premium payments are automatically made.

After hiding unneeded columns, the summary of the impact of the employer's proposal can be printed for review by the union negotiating committee, as shown below. Employees' annual contributions would increase by nearly $100,000 from

$66,120 to $164,029; all employees would now be contributing; and the average Cost per Hour for contributors in 2011 would be $1.21. The spreadsheet also shows the impact on groups of employees in individual categories, with P-T employees choosing family indemnity coverage paying $380.55 per month in 2011.

	A	C	D	H	I	M	N	R	S
1	RMC Proposal #1 - Health Insurance								
2		2008		2009		2010		2011	
3	Type of Health Coverage	Employee's Monthly Premium	Employer's Monthly Premium	Employee's Monthly Premium	Employer's Monthly Premium	Employee's Monthly Premium	Employer's Monthly Premium	Employee's Monthly Premium	Employer's Monthly Premium
4	Indemnity Plan								
5	Single Employee	$0.00	$327.40	$32.74	$327.40	$61.55	$327.40	$81.00	$327.40
6	Family	$90.00	$720.62	$171.06	$720.62	$242.40	$720.62	$290.55	$720.62
7	Single + 1 Dependent	$60.00	$542.90	$120.29	$542.90	$173.35	$542.90	$209.16	$542.90
8	P-T Single Employee	$90.00	$237.40	$122.74	$237.40	$151.55	$237.40	$171.00	$237.40
9	P-T Family	$180.00	$630.62	$261.06	$630.62	$332.40	$630.62	$380.55	$630.62
10	P-T Single + 1 Dependent	$120.00	$482.90	$180.29	$482.90	$233.35	$482.90	$269.16	$482.90
15	HMO Plan								
16	Single Employee	$0.00	$247.74	$14.86	$247.74	$30.62	$247.74	$47.32	$247.74
17	Family	$70.00	$491.62	$103.70	$491.62	$139.42	$491.62	$177.28	$491.62
18	Single + 1 Dependent	$50.00	$376.68	$75.60	$376.68	$102.74	$376.68	$131.50	$376.68
19	P-T Single Employee	$70.00	$177.74	$84.86	$177.74	$100.62	$177.74	$117.32	$177.74
20	P-T Family	$140.00	$421.62	$173.70	$421.62	$209.42	$421.62	$247.28	$421.62
21	P-T Single + 1 Dependent	$100.00	$326.68	$125.60	$326.68	$152.74	$326.68	$181.50	$326.68
22	EMPLOYER'S TOTAL MONTHLY COST		$32,498.12		$32,498.12		$32,498.12		$32,498.12
23	EMPLOYER'S ANNUAL COST		$389,977.44		$389,977.44		$389,977.44		$389,977.44
24	ANNUAL COST PER EMPLOYEE		$4,062.27		$4,062.27		$4,062.27		$4,062.27
25	AVERAGE COST PER HOUR		$2.43		$2.43		$2.43		$2.43
26	Enrolled employees								
27	Employees' Total Monthly Contributions	$5,510.00		$8,428.23		$11,234.58		$13,669.13	
28	Employees' Annual Contributions	$66,120.00		$101,138.80		$134,814.90		$164,029.52	
29	Average Cost Per Employee Contributing	$1,049.52		$1,248.63		$1,664.38		$2,025.06	
30	Average Employee Contribution Per Hour	$0.63		$0.75		$1.00		$1.21	

Shift Differentials

The employer proposes to set the shift differential for 2nd shift at 6% and for 3rd shift at 10%. What is the impact on those shift workers and the overall bargaining unit? The union could cost this proposal for 2008 to see what the difference would have been in that year and then project the impact for 2009 and 2010 using both the union's wage proposal and the employer's wage proposal.

The methodology is straightforward in the Hourly Wage-Related Premium Payments worksheet since there is already space for percentage hourly shift differentials. Cells B18 and C18 are formatted as Percent and the employer's proposals (6% and 10%) are entered for each shift. The number of employees and average hours worked can be entered or copied from the cells above. The average hourly wage is entered as AveST08 and a formula for calculating the ANNUAL COST for the 2nd shift is entered as follows in cell B22= B18*B19*B20*B21. It can be copied for 3rd shift.

The total costs for shift differentials in 2008, had the employer's proposal been in effect, is the sum of 2nd and 3rd shift and would total $81,005 – a considerable savings for the employer from the current cost of $124,493. The cost can be projected for 2009 and 2010 using the employer's wage proposal by using AveST09 and AveST10 in cells F19 and F20. The union may want to make a more accurate estimate of the actual hourly wages of employees on shift work but in the absence of doing so, the average wage is likely a very good proxy.

	A	B	C	E	F	G
1	RMC Proposal #1 - Hourly Wage-Related Premium Payments					
11	Shift Differentials	2nd Shift	3rd Shift	TOTAL SD COST	2009	2010
12	Flat Hourly Shift Differentials	$ 1.50	$ 2.75			
13	Number of Employees Receiving	24	14			
14	Average Number of Hours Worked	1671	1671			
15	ANNUAL COST	$ 60,157.87	$ 64,335.50	$124,493.37		
16	ANNUAL COST PER EMPLOYEE			$1,296.81		
17	AVERAGE COST PER HOUR			$0.78		
18	Percentage Hourly Shift Differential	6.00%	10.00%			
19	Average Hourly Wage	$17.07	$17.07		$18.06	$18.62
20	Number of Employees Receiving	24	14			
21	Average Number of Hours Worked	1671	1671			
22	ANNUAL COST	$41,072.98	$39,932.06	$81,005.05	$85,685.56	$88,370.92
23	ANNUAL COST PER EMPLOYEE	$427.84	$415.96	$843.80	$892.56	$920.53
24	AVERAGE COST PER HOUR	$0.26	$0.25	$0.50	$0.53	$0.55

The union negotiating committee thinks that getting shift differentials established as a percentage of hourly wage is not a bad idea, albeit at a rate that will not disadvantage current shift workers. So it would like to see what the average cost would be if these percentage shift differentials were used, along with the union's wage proposal. To do so, the entire block *from the employer's proposal* (B18 to G18, down to B24 to G24) is copied and pasted into the Union Proposal #1 workbook. Excel will provide a message that AveST wages for each year as well as TotEmp and PHrs have already been defined in the *destination workbook* and asks if these are to be used in the destination workbook. The answer is yes, and very quickly the union committee has the comparison shown below, using its wage proposal and the 6% and 10% shift differentials.

Even when using the union's wage proposal it is clear that accepting 6% and 10% shift differentials would not be favorable to the shift employees. Obviously, it is easy to calculate the current percentage value of the shift differentials as $1.50/$17.07 (about 8.8%) and $2.75/$17.07 (about 16.1%) but setting up the spreadsheet will allow the union committee to do several 'what if' scenarios by just changing the percentages in cells B18 and C18 – along with *its wage proposal* – to find the breakeven point for 2009 and 2010.

	A	B	C	E	F	G
1	Union Proposal #1 - Hourly Wage-Related Premium Payments					
11	Shift Differentials	2nd Shift	3rd Shift	TOTAL SD COST	2009	2010
12	Flat Hourly Shift Differentials	$ 1.50	$ 2.75			
13	Number of Employees Receiving	24	14			
14	Average Number of Hours Worked	1671	1671			
15	ANNUAL COST	$ 60,157.87	$ 64,335.50	$124,493.37		
16	ANNUAL COST PER EMPLOYEE			$1,296.81		
17	AVERAGE COST PER HOUR			$0.78		
18	Percentage Hourly Shift Differential	6.00%	10.00%			
19	Average Hourly Wage	$17.07	$17.07		$18.45	$19.38
20	Number of Employees Receiving	24	14			
21	Average Number of Hours Worked	1671	1671			
22	ANNUAL COST	$41,072.98	$39,932.06	$81,005.05	$87,557.67	$91,986.73
23	ANNUAL COST PER EMPLOYEE	$427.84	$415.96	$843.80	$912.06	$958.20
24	AVERAGE COST PER HOUR	$0.26	$0.25	$0.50	$0.55	$0.57

Vacations

The employer proposed a third week of vacation for employees with 6 but less than 15 years of service. The union must modify the count of employees in each category that it created in the Data from the Employer worksheet. This can be easily done by inserting Auto Sums for the appropriate years of service and then the number of eligible full-time and part-time employees can be linked to the Vacation worksheet. With these links entered, the AVERAGE COST PER HOUR is automatically calculated, based on the employer's wage proposal. The following screen shot shows the costs of the employer's vacation proposal for 2009 based on the employer's wage proposal.

	A	E	F	G	H	I	J
19	RMC Proposal #1 - Vacation Pay						
20		2008			2009		
21	Number of Days or Weeks of Vacation for Each Category	SUBTOTAL COST	Number of Days or Weeks of Vacation for Each Category	Number of Hours Paid	Number of Eligible Employees	Vacation Pay Rate	SUBTOTAL COST
22	Full-time employees		Full-time employees				
23	2		2	80	9		
24	3		3	120	34		
25	4		4	160	7		
26	5		5	200	2		
27	Subtotal	$104,095.95	Subtotal		6320	$19.76	$124,863.79
28	Part-time employees		Part-time employees				
29	2		2	60	11		
30	3		3	90	26		
31	4		4	120	7		
32	5		5	150	0		
33	Subtotal	$52,599.29	Subtotal		3840	$16.04	$61,608.19
34	Total Hours of Paid Vacation:		Total Hours of Paid Vacation:		10160		
35	ANNUAL COST		ANNUAL COST			$186,471.97	
36	ANNUAL COST PER E	$1,632.24	ANNUAL COST PER EMPLOYEE				$1,942.42
37	AVERAGE COST PER	$0.98	AVERAGE COST PER HOUR				$1.16

Summary of Regional Medical Center Proposal #1

The summary worksheet of the employer's proposal will be partially completed since the links created within the Union Proposal workbook exist here as well. But because the employer has not made any proposal to increase the number of holidays or personal days and proposed to substitute the percent shift differentials (at a lower cost) and made it clear that it would consider *either* a longevity increase *or* the increment increase, these adjustments must be made within the Employer Proposal #1 workbook.

For holidays, it is simple: revert back to only 10 holidays in the formulas in cells G5 and M5. For personal days, modify the formulas for both full-time employees and part-time employees to continue with only 3 days and 2 days respectively. For longevity, change the formula back to 1%. By making only these 3-minute changes, the rest of the worksheet remains intact and the roll-up costs for these benefits based on the *employer's wage and increment proposal* are calculated for 2009 and 2010.

For the employer's proposal on shift differentials, the costs for 2009 and 2010 in the percentage shift differentials part of that worksheet need to be linked to the summary page in the appropriate row and the flat shift differential costs deleted for 2009 and 2010. These adjustments have been made to the Summary of Costs for the employer's proposal and can be seen in that workbook.

It may be extremely useful for the union committee to see a side-by-side comparison of the employer's proposal with the union's proposal. To do that, add one more worksheet to the Union Proposal workbook.

Excel Basics – Adding another worksheet
To the right of the tab for the last worksheet (Data from the Employer) is an icon that easily permits adding another worksheet with just a click. After the worksheet is created, the tab can be renamed by right-clicking, choosing rename from the drop-down menu and typing in the new name, which in this case is called Comparisons.

All the information from the Summary of Costs worksheet in the Union Proposal #1 workbook can be copied and pasted into cell A1 of the new Comparison worksheet. The next step is to copy the information in the RMC Proposal #1 Summary of Costs and paste it in the same rows in the Comparison worksheet beginning in cell H3. **A caution here!** If the block, including formulas and named cells, is pasted, Excel will advise that the same cell names, for instance AveST09, PHrs, etc. have been used in both workbooks. It will ask if these cells should be renamed and that is one possibility. But the better solution is to again choose Paste Special and then just paste the *values* from the Employer Proposal #1 worksheet. They are not going to change – they are what they are. When another proposal is made by the employer a new workbook can be created to incorporate the modifications in its proposal. After a few new column titles and a few borders, the comparison of union and employer proposals #1 for 2009 and 2010 looks like the screen shot on the next page.

In percentage terms there is quite a large difference in the union's first year proposal (8.82%) and the employer's (4.19%). In the second year, the difference between the employer's and union's proposals is slightly narrower.

But if the employer were to agree to the union's proposal to increase the step increment from 1.8% to 2.0% in 2009 and then apply its wage increases of $.40 in 2009 and $.30 in 2010, the value of the employer's *wage proposal* in the two years is perhaps in the realm of possible agreement. The employer's proposed change in hourly shift differentials is problematic as is the employer's shifting of health insurance premium increases entirely to the employees. And the union's health insurance proposal, as currently calculated, does not reflect any of the increases in premiums.

	A	B	C	D	E	F	G	H	I
1	Comparison of Proposals #1 - Summary of Costs								
2						Union Proposal #1		RMC Proposal #1	
3	Type of Fringe Benefit		TOTAL ANNUAL COST	ANNUAL COST PER EMPLOYEE	AVERAGE COST PER HOUR 2008	2009	2010	2009	2010
4	Straight-Time (Base) Hourly Wage				$17.07	$18.45	$19.38	$18.06	$18.62
5	Daily/Weekly Overtime Premiums				$0.29	$0.32	$0.33	$0.31	$0.32
6	Flat Hourly Shift Differentials				$0.78	$0.78	$0.78		
7	Percentage Hourly Shift Differentials							$0.53	$0.55
10	Paid Holidays Not Worked				$0.85	$1.01	$1.06	$0.90	$0.93
11	Personal Days				$0.21	$0.37	$0.39	$0.22	$0.23
12	Sick Leave				$0.39	$0.42	$0.44	$0.41	$0.43
13	Bereavement Leave				$0.02	$0.02	$0.02	$0.02	$0.02
17	Vacations				$0.96	$1.23	$1.29	$1.16	$1.20
18	Health Insurance				$2.43	$2.57	$2.57	$2.43	$2.43
19	Dental Insurance				$0.73	$0.73	$0.73	$0.73	$0.73
20	Life Insurance				$0.18	$0.18	$0.18	$0.18	$0.18
23	Tuition Reimbursement				$0.07	$0.07	$0.07	$0.07	$0.07
26	Longevity Annual Payments				$0.04	$0.12	$0.14	$0.06	$0.07
27	Defined Benefit Pension Contribution				$1.40	$1.40	$1.40	$1.40	$1.40
31	TOTAL LABOR COST	$4,077,179	$42,470.61	$25.42	$27.66	$28.79	$26.48	$27.17	
32									
33	Sum of Roll-Up Contractual Benefits				$2.77	$3.49	$3.68	$3.62	$3.75
34	Roll-Up Factor				16.2%	18.9%	19.0%	20.1%	20.1%
35									
36	Percent Increase Each Year					8.82%	4.08%	4.19%	2.60%

Union Proposal #2

The union decides to modify its proposal for the next negotiating session. The union is willing to reduce its first year wage proposal to 3.5% if the employer will agree to increase the step increment from 1.8% to 2.0%. The union also says the increment increase can be applied before the general wage increase if that is what the employer wants. For health insurance the union counter proposes that it would like to maintain the current premium payments made by employees to both plans rather than reducing them as originally proposed. It rejects the employer's shift differential proposal but says it is willing to consider 7% and 14% in the second year of the contract. As its last counterproposal it says that with an agreement on wages and the increment increase it will shift the one additional holiday into the second year and drop its proposals for an increase in the number of personal leave days and longevity pay. Of course, the union committee had already made an estimate of the costs of its counterproposal. Here is what the committee did.

The entire workbook for Union Proposal #1 was saved as Union Proposal #2 and the following modifications were made. For wages, the union simply changed the % increase in cell F4 from 1.045 to 1.035 in the formula bar and hit Enter. It then copied that formula and pasted it into cells F22, F40, F58 and F76. Its work was done on the wage counterproposal and the wage calculations were already in the Summary Page and included in the roll-up costs.

Health insurance was not quite as easy. The union copied the employer's proposal and pasted it into the union's second proposal workbook because it had the projected premium increases for three years. So the values in the block of cells for 2009 (G2 to J2, down to G31 to J31) were deleted from the Union Proposal #2 worksheet. Then the whole block of cells from the Employer's Proposal #1 for all three years were copied and pasted into cell G2. The union now had a mirror image of the employer's health insurance proposal.

Next the employee contribution amounts from 2008 were copied and pasted into the next three years as *values*, the formula for the employer's contribution (total premium minus employee premium) was copied from cell D5 and pasted into I5, N5 and S5 for the indemnity plan and into I16, N16 and S16 for the HMO plan and the formula was copied down the column with Auto Fill. In a few quick steps the union knew the costs of its second health insurance proposal: the employer's costs would go up from $2.43 to $2.65 in 2009, to $2.86 in 2010 and to $3.04 in 2011 and the employees' average hourly contributions would remain at $.63 for the 63 employees contributing. Since the union's proposal workbook did not have these values linked to the Summary of Costs worksheet for 2009-2011, it was now done.

For shift differentials, the union committee decided that if its wage and increment proposal was accepted by the employer the 7% and 14% shift differentials in the second year would have a negligible impact on the shift employees. Making the calculation was rather straightforward. In Union Proposal #2, in the Hourly-Related Wage Premiums worksheet, the union continued the flat shift differentials into 2009 and entered 7% and 14% as the percentage shift differentials for 2010. Based on its proposed average wages in 2010, the cost to the employer (and value to the shift employees) would be similar to 2008 ($.73 versus the flat $.79), as shown in the screen shot below. Cell G24 was named AveSD10 – the average shift differential cost for that year.

	A	B	C	E	F	G
1	**Union Proposal #2 - Hourly Wage-Related Premium Payments**					
11	Shift Differentials	2nd Shift	3rd Shift	TOTAL SD COST	2009	2010
12	Flat Hourly Shift Differentials	$ 1.50	$ 2.75			
13	Number of Employees Receiving	24	14			
14	Average Number of Hours Worked	1671	1671			
15	ANNUAL COST	$ 60,157.87	$ 64,335.50	$124,493.37		
16	ANNUAL COST PER EMPLOYEE			$1,296.81		
17	AVERAGE COST PER HOUR			$0.78	$0.78	
18	Percentage Hourly Shift Differential	7.00%	14.00%			
19	Average Hourly Wage	$17.07	$17.07		$18.27	$19.20
20	Number of Employees Receiving	24	14			
21	Average Number of Hours Worked	1671	1671			
22	ANNUAL COST	$47,918.48	$55,904.89	$103,823.37	$111,147.91	$116,770.26
23	ANNUAL COST PER EMPLOYEE	$499.15	$582.34	$1,081.49	$1,157.79	$1,216.36
24	AVERAGE COST PER HOUR	$0.30	$0.35	**$0.65**	**$0.69**	**$0.73**

For its modified holiday proposal, the union changed 11 holidays in 2009 back to 10 in the formula in cell G5 and left it as 11 in cell M5 for 2010. It also changed the rate paid for holidays in 2010 in cell L5 to =AveST10+AveSD10. The revised figures are now in the Summary of Costs worksheet. Lastly, the union changed the longevity pay formula back to 1%.

The union committee wants to see its new proposal side-by-side with its first proposal and the employer's proposal. But, there would be a problem with the Comparison worksheet since Excel updated what was Union Proposal #1 with the modifications from Union Proposal #2. What to do? Not too tough of a problem. The summary statistics from Union Proposal #1 can be copied and pasted into the Comparison worksheet as *values*. And the summary statistics from Union Proposal #2 can also be copied and pasted into the Comparison worksheet as *values*.

As seen in the screen shot below, there is still a considerable difference between the union's new proposal and what the employer has on the table but it has narrowed.

Contract Costing for Union Negotiators

A	E	F	G	H	I	J	K
Comparison of Proposals - Summary of Costs							
		UP #1		RMC Prop #1		UP #2	
Type of Fringe Benefit	AVE COST PER HOUR 9/2008	2009	2010	2009	2010	2009	2010
Straight-Time (Base) Hourly Wage	$17.07	$18.45	$19.38	$18.06	$18.62	$18.27	$19.20
Daily/Weekly Overtime Premiums	$0.29	$0.32	$0.33	$0.31	$0.32	$0.31	$0.33
Flat Hourly Shift Differentials	$0.78	$0.78	$0.78			$0.78	
% Hourly Shift Differentials				$0.53	$0.55		$0.73
Paid Holidays Not Worked	$0.85	$1.01	$1.06	$0.90	$0.93	$0.91	$1.05
Personal Days	$0.21	$0.37	$0.39	$0.22	$0.23	$0.23	$0.24
Sick Leave	$0.39	$0.42	$0.44	$0.41	$0.43	$0.42	$0.44
Bereavement Leave	$0.02	$0.02	$0.02	$0.02	$0.02	$0.02	$0.02
Vacations	$0.96	$1.23	$1.29	$1.16	$1.20	$1.22	$1.28
Health Insurance	$2.43	$2.57	$2.57	$2.43	$2.43	$2.65	$2.86
Dental Insurance	$0.73	$0.73	$0.73	$0.73	$0.73	$0.73	$0.73
Life Insurance	$0.18	$0.18	$0.18	$0.18	$0.18	$0.18	$0.18
Tuition Reimbursement	$0.07	$0.07	$0.07	$0.07	$0.07	$0.07	$0.07
Longevity Annual Payments	$0.04	$0.12	$0.14	$0.06	$0.07	$0.06	$0.07
Defined Benefit Pension Contribution	$1.40	$1.40	$1.40	$1.40	$1.40	$1.40	$1.40
TOTAL LABOR COST	$25.42	$27.66	$28.79	$26.48	$27.17	$27.24	$28.58
Sum of Roll-Up Contractual Benefits	$2.77	$3.49	$3.68	$3.62	$3.75	$3.17	$4.16
Roll-Up Factor	16.2%	18.9%	19.0%	20.1%	20.1%	17.3%	21.7%
Percent Increase Each Year		8.82%	4.08%	4.19%	2.60%	7.16%	4.95%

Regional Medical Center Proposal #2

After several more negotiating sessions, the RMC offers a second proposal. It agrees to increase the increment increase from 1.8% to 2.0% at the beginning of the new contract and to then apply a $.60 wage increase across the board in the first year since the union said it did not care which was done first. It also draws the union's attention to the fact that the RMC considers 60 cents as essentially equivalent to the union's proposal for a 3.5% increase, based on an average straight-time wage of $17.07 on 9/1/08.

The RMC also offers a $.40 across the board increase in the second year. The RMC says it will withdraw its proposal on health insurance premium sharing and it will agree with the union's proposal to continue the same employee contributions to the health care plan over the term of a new contract if the union agrees with its wage proposal. The RMC also says it would agree to the union's proposals for one additional holiday in the second year and to change to 7% and 14% shift differentials in the second year. But it makes this contingent on the union's agreement to totally withdraw its proposal on personal days. It also says it is standing firm on its vacation proposal.

The union committee has some analyzing and tough decisions ahead of it. RMC Proposal #1 workbook is saved with a new name, RMC Proposal #2, and the following modifications are made to correspond with these new proposals.

In column G of the Average Wage with Progression worksheet, the wage increase for 2009 is changed from $.40 to $.60 and for 2010 from $.30 to $.40. No change is made for 2011. In the Hourly Wage-Related Premiums worksheet, all the Percent Shift Differential information for the second year (cells B18 to G18, down to B24 to G24), are cleared and the same cells from Union Proposal #2 are copied and pasted as a block into cell B18. Excel asks if the named cells in the destination worksheet should be retained and the answer to all is yes. The union's shift differential proposal is now part of the employer's proposal.

Excel Basics – Clearing or deleting cells?
There is a difference in Excel between clearing and deleting. If you want to remove the contents of a cell (or row or column), you select that cell, row or column and then right click and choose the instruction 'Clear Contents'. The values or formulas are cleared but the cell, row or column continues to exist in the worksheet. If you choose Delete from that drop down menu the cell, row or column will actually be removed from the worksheet. When you choose that second option, Excel will ask how you want to shift the remaining cells, rows or columns. However, using the Delete **key** on the keyboard while working in Excel will simply clear the contents of the cell, row or column that has been selected; they will not be removed from the worksheet.

For holidays, the union simply changes the number of holidays in the formula for the second year (cell M5) from 10 to 11. Health insurance is not much more complicated. All the data in the Health & Life Insurance worksheet in RMC Proposal #2 is cleared in a block from cell G4 to U4, down to G31 to U31. Then going to the same worksheet in Union Proposal #2, the same block of cells is copied and pasted into cell G4, accepting the destination named cells for TotEmp and PHrs.

The union's work is essentially done other than to check the Summary of Costs worksheet. Everything seems to have updated correctly except that the cost of the now-flat shift differentials for 2009 needs to be set equal to 2008 and the percent shift differential for 2009 needs to be cleared. The cost of the shift differential for 2010, based on the union's proposal of 7% and 14% and the employer's wage proposal, seems to be incorporated properly in the summary.

The union committee now wants to see a comparison with the previous proposals. The data in the Summary of Costs worksheet of RMC Proposal #2 are copied and pasted as *values* into the Comparison worksheet in the union's own Proposal #2 workbook. Here is how the comparison looks.

Comparison of Proposals - Summary of Costs

	AVE COST PER HOUR	UP #1		RMC Prop #1		UP #2		RMC Prop #2	
Type of Fringe Benefit	2008	2009	2010	2009	2010	2009	2010	2009	2010
Straight-Time (Base) Hourly W	$17.07	$18.45	$19.38	$18.06	$18.62	$18.27	$19.20	$18.26	$18.92
Daily/Weekly Overtime Pre	$0.29	$0.32	$0.33	$0.31	$0.32	$0.31	$0.33	$0.31	$0.32
Flat Hourly Shift Differentials	$0.78	$0.78	$0.78			$0.78		$0.78	
% Hourly Shift Differentials				$0.53	$0.55		$0.73		$0.72
Paid Holidays Not Worked	$0.85	$1.01	$1.06	$0.90	$0.93	$0.91	$1.05	$0.91	$1.04
Personal Days	$0.21	$0.37	$0.39	$0.22	$0.23	$0.23	$0.24	$0.23	$0.23
Sick Leave	$0.39	$0.42	$0.44	$0.41	$0.43	$0.42	$0.44	$0.42	$0.43
Bereavement Leave	$0.02	$0.02	$0.02	$0.02	$0.02	$0.02	$0.02	$0.02	$0.02
Vacations	$0.96	$1.23	$1.29	$1.16	$1.20	$1.22	$1.28	$1.18	$1.22
Health Insurance	$2.43	$2.57	$2.57	$2.43	$2.43	$2.65	$2.86	$2.65	$2.86
Dental Insurance	$0.73	$0.73	$0.73	$0.73	$0.73	$0.73	$0.73	$0.73	$0.73
Life Insurance	$0.18	$0.18	$0.18	$0.18	$0.18	$0.18	$0.18	$0.18	$0.18
Tuition Reimbursement	$0.07	$0.07	$0.07	$0.07	$0.07	$0.07	$0.07	$0.07	$0.07
Longevity Annual Paymen	$0.04	$0.12	$0.14	$0.06	$0.07	$0.06	$0.07	$0.06	$0.07
Defined Benefit Pension Cont	$1.40	$1.40	$1.40	$1.40	$1.40	$1.40	$1.40	$1.40	$1.40
TOTAL LABOR COST	$25.42	$27.66	$28.79	$26.48	$27.17	$27.24	$28.58	$27.17	$28.21
Sum of Roll-Up Contractual B	$2.77	$3.49	$3.68	$3.62	$3.75	$3.17	$4.16	$3.12	$4.06
Roll-Up Factor	16.2%	18.9%	19.0%	20.1%	20.1%	17.3%	21.7%	17.1%	21.4%
Percent Increase Each Year		8.82%	4.08%	4.19%	2.60%	7.16%	4.95%	6.92%	3.81%

The parties are quite close to each other on the first year wage increase despite the differing approaches of a flat increase versus a percentage wage increase. The union reasons that with the increment increase, a flat increase is probably fairer to employees at lower wage levels. It examines the impact of both its last proposal and the RMC's last proposal on average wages for both full-time and part-time employees and doesn't see any particularly disparate treatment.

Getting the health insurance continuance without any additional cost to the employees is significant. Shifting the additional holiday to the second year as the union had proposed seems ok. The remaining issues appear to be the change in the shift differentials in the second year (an average benefit/cost of $.06 less for shift employees) and the differing vacation proposals (also with a difference in average cost of $.06).

The union decides to try to make a trade-off at the next negotiating session. If the employer will accept a new proposal on shift differentials that will not disadvantage shift employees, the union will accept the employer's proposal on vacations as well as the rest of the package on the table. So what percentage should the union propose for shift differentials in 2010? The union tries various percentages in cells B17 and B18 in the RMC Proposal #2 workbook to see what percentage proposal (keeping the 2 to 1 ratio between 3rd shift and 2nd shift) would yield around $.78 in average cost to the employer. Proposing 7.5% for 2nd shift and 15% for 3rd shift yields an average cost of $.77 in 2010 based on the employer's last wage proposal.

At the next negotiating session the union is prepared to lay out its proposal for settlement of all outstanding issues over a two-year term:
- An increase in the increment between all wage steps from 1.8% to 2.0%; then a wage increase of $.60 across the board in the first year; an across the board wage increase of $.40 in 2010.
- No change in shift differentials in the first year and 7.5% for the 2nd shift and 15% for 3rd shift in 2010.
- The employer will maintain existing health insurance plans, employee premium payments will be frozen and the employer will be responsible for all premium increases.
- Employees with six or more years of service but less than 15 will receive a 3rd week of vacation in the first contract year.
- One additional holiday in the second year of the agreement.

The Final Agreement

At the next negotiating session, after the normal bantering, the union presents its proposal and the Regional Medical Center says, after a little bit of fussing, that the union has a new two-year agreement.

Though the negotiating parties are finished, this manual must deal with the issue of productive hours for 2009 and 2010. They did change slightly due the larger number of employees eligible for the 3rd week of vacation in 2009 and because of the 11th holiday added in 2010. The Average Productive Hours per Employee in 2008 were 1,671 and will fall in 2009 to 1,659 and to 1,651 in 2010. In theory, the parties should adjust the Summary of Costs worksheet of the final agreement to incorporate these changes – but both sides of the negotiating table are quite tired and decide to leave the task to two years hence when they begin their preparations for the next round of negotiations.

The parties do agree that a joint document on the overall value of the tentative agreement can be prepared for the union members and for RMC senior management comparing September 2008 with January 2009 and 2010. The union says sure – not a problem. A few columns containing the earlier proposals are hidden, a few rows are added to show full-time employees' average wages and part-time employees' average wages and here is how the Final Agreement from the union's Comparison worksheet looks:

	A	E	N	O
1	**Comparison of Proposals - Summary of Costs**			
2			Final Agreement of the Negotiating Committees	
3	Type of Fringe Benefit	AVE COST PER HOUR 9/2008	January 1, 2009	January 1, 2010
4	Straight-Time (Base) Hourly Wage	$17.07	$18.26	$18.92
5	Daily/Weekly Overtime Premiums	$0.29	$0.31	$0.32
6	Flat Hourly Shift Differentials	$0.78	$0.78	
7	% Hourly Shift Differentials			$0.77
10	Paid Holidays Not Worked	$0.85	$0.91	$1.04
11	Personal Days	$0.21	$0.23	$0.23
12	Sick Leave	$0.39	$0.42	$0.43
13	Bereavement Leave	$0.02	$0.02	$0.02
17	Vacations	$0.96	$1.18	$1.22
18	Health Insurance	$2.43	$2.65	$2.86
19	Dental Insurance	$0.73	$0.73	$0.73
20	Life Insurance	$0.18	$0.18	$0.18
23	Tuition Reimbursement	$0.07	$0.07	$0.07
26	Longevity Annual Payments	$0.04	$0.06	$0.07
27	Defined Benefit Pension Contribution	$1.40	$1.40	$1.40
31	TOTAL LABOR COST	$25.42	$27.17	$28.26
32				
33	Sum of Roll-Up Contractual Benefits	$2.77	$3.12	$4.11
34	Roll-Up Factor	16.2%	17.1%	21.7%
35				
36	Percent Increase Each Year		6.92%	4.00%
37				
38	Average Wage for F-T Employees	$18.72	$19.96	$20.63
39	Average Wage for P-T Employees	$15.11	$16.24	$16.90

A Last Point

Some readers surely noticed the union's *strategic mistake* when it said it didn't care whether the wage increase or the increment increase was implemented first. From the union's perspective of a percent increase in the first year, it truly would not have made any difference. But since the RMC was proposing a flat across the board wage, it certainly does make a difference. Need proof? Make yourself a little spreadsheet!

Appendix

Sample Letter Requesting Information for Collective Bargaining[1]

Date

[To appropriate employer official]

Dear _____:

For the union to prepare for re-negotiation of our collective agreement we request the following information:

1. Wages. The number of employees in each wage classification [or steps of each classification] as of [date]. If there are any "red-circled" employees, employees receiving bonuses, merit premiums or any other supplements to the wage rates in the collective agreement, please provide the appropriate information for these employees, by name.
2. Years of service. A current seniority list providing date of hire and/or a compilation of employees categorized by years of service.[2]
3. Hours of work. Please provide the number of straight-time hours paid for all employees for the period [from _____ to _____] and the number of overtime hours paid for each type[3] of overtime premium and other premium hours worked (e.g. holidays worked) covered by the collective agreement for the same time period.
4. Shift differentials. The number of employees currently assigned to each shift.
5. Other wage differentials. The names and number of employees receiving any other contractual hourly wage differentials, by type.
6. Other contractual benefits. The total annual cost for the period [from _____ to _____] for the following:
    a. Bereavement leave
    b. Jury duty leave
    c. Sick leave
    d. Personal days
    e. Leave for union business
    f. Severance pay
    g. Tool allowances
    h. Tuition reimbursement
    i. [add or delete in accord with your contract]
7. Insurance plans.
    a. The number of employees participating in each health insurance plan[4] and categories of coverage and the current premium cost for each plan and

categories of coverage. If projected premium increases are available at this time, please provide that information.

    b. The number of employees participating in the [dental plan, vision care plan, etc.] and the current premium cost for each plan. If projected premium increases are available at this time, please provide that information

    c. The annual or monthly cost for life insurance and AD&D coverage for covered employees.

    d. The annual or monthly cost for the short-term disability (S&A) plan for covered employees.

8. A copy of the most current actuarial report on the pension plan, the most current report of the plan's trustees and the most current reports filed with the US Department of Labor regarding administration of the plan and the amount contributed by the employer for the previous plan year.

9. The employer's contribution to employees' 401(k) accounts for the period [from _____ to _____]

If it is possible to supply this information, or parts of it, in electronic form, for instance in Excel worksheets, please feel free to do so. If any of this information cannot be provided within two weeks from receipt of this letter, please contact the undersigned so that we can discuss any questions, concerns or problems and agree on a time frame and a sequence for receiving the information.

Sincerely,
[Union representative]

---

[1] This is simply a sample and the union negotiating committee should modify the letter to correspond to its particular contract and its benefits. It only covers items that are mandatory subjects for bargaining and presumptively relevant for negotiations. Certainly the union can consider requesting information such as a current income statement, a balance sheet, business and operating plans, budgets, forecasts or any other documents dealing with projected revenue, costs and operating results. These are generally not considered presumptively relevant to bargaining.

[2] Whether you need other specific information about members of the bargaining unit should be considered: for instance, birth date or age; family status; number of dependents, actual date of hire. You should not request information that the union already has. If you have an up-to-date seniority list, the union can prepare a spreadsheet with categories. Your goal is to get information needed for the upcoming negotiations, not to harass the employer.

[3] You should list the specific types of overtime premiums contained in your contract, for instance 6th or 7th day premiums, call-ins, etc.

[4] Bargaining over health care plans can be quite contentious and difficult in the current environment of skyrocketing premiums. However, it is not recommended that the union request items such as experience rating by categories of coverage (e.g. hospitalizations, physicians visits, pharmacy, etc.) or a detailed breakdown of premiums costs (e.g. for claims, profit margin, broker fees, retention, etc) in its initial information request. These items can be the subject of a follow up request during the course of negotiations if the negotiators need to work on re-designing the health insurance plans.

Index

#

########. *See* Adjust column width
#VALUE!. *See* Warning and error messages

A

Accept icon, *11*
Actuarial evaluation
  defined benefit plan, 56
Adding new worksheet
  how to, 83
Adjust column width
  how to, 20
Align text or numbers
  how to, 18
Annual percent increase
  formula, 74
Auto Fit Column Width function, 68
Auto Sum function
  how to use, 16
Auto Sum function ∑ icon, *13*
AutoFill command
  how to use, 14
AveFT
  named cell, 41
AvePT
  named cell, 41
Average Annual Cost per Employee
  defined, 6
Average Cost per Employee per Hour
  defined, 7
Average straight-time wage rate
  defined, *11*
AveST
  named cell, 32

B

Bereavement leaves, 43
Best Fit function
  how to use. *See* Adjust column width
Blank Workbook, 4
Block of cells
  copying and pasting, 21
Borders, 78

C

Cell display format, 18
Cell reference formula, 30
Clearing cells, 88

Clicking-in formulas and cells
  how to, *13*
Column margins
  adjusting, 68
Columns, inserting and deleting
  how to, 19
Comments in cells
  inserting, viewing, 34
Comparison of proposals
  Union #1 and RMC#1, 83
Copying cells
  how to, *14*
Copying/pasting values
  how to, 72
Creep. *See* Roll-up benefits
Ctrl ~ function, 68
Currency Format, 18

D

Decimal point
  increasing or decreasing. *See* Cell display format
Defined benefit pension plan, 56
Defined contribution pension plan, 56
Delete key on keyboard, 88
Deleting cells, 88
Deleting rows
  how to, 19
Dental insurance, 51
Destination workbook, 81

E

Employer's duty to provide information, 8
Error messages. *See* Warning and error messages

F

Fill handle, 23
  how to use, 15
Final agreement, 90
Flashing marquee. *See* Auto Sum function
Flat wage increase
  RMC proposal #1, 76
FORMAT FOLDER
  on CD, 4
Format Workbook
  on CD, 4
Format Worksheet #1, *11*
Format Worksheet #2, 21
Format Worksheet #3, 27
Format Worksheet #4, 31

Format Worksheet #5, 40
Format Worksheet #6, 44
Format Worksheet #7
    dental insurance, 52
    health insurance, 49
    life insurance/disability insurance, 55
Format worksheet #8, 57
Format Worksheet #8
    pension plans and SUB, 58
Format Worksheet #9, 60
Formatting pages for printing, 78
Formatting tools
    how to use, 18
Formula Bar, *11*
Formulas in Excel
    essentials, *13*

G

General Format, 18

H

Health insurance
    Average Cost per Contributing Employee, 50
    employee and employer premiums, 49
    family status, 48
Health insurance plans, 48
Hide rows and columns
    how to, 38
Holidays not worked
    caveats, 39

I

Impact cost. *See* Roll-up benefits
Increment increase
    union proposal #1, 65
Increment increase formula
    how to construct, 23
Information request
    cost of assembling data, 9
    electronic format, *9*
    filing NLRB charge, 9
    in writing, 8
    verbally, 8
    when to send, 7
Insert a new row
    how to, 17

J

Jury duty leave, 43

L

Life insurance
    based on income, 53
    flat amount, 53
Linking worksheets. *See* Referencing cells
Links
    to summary page, 60
Longevity pay, 58

M

Merge & Center
    how to, 19
Mirror image block, 72
Modifying worksheet data
    how to, *11*
Moving between worksheets
    how to, 29
Multi-employer pension plan, 56
Multiplying fringes. *See* Roll-up benefits

N

Named cells
    in destination worksheet, 88
Naming cells
    how to, 28
New worksheet
    adding, 83
Notice to reopen and renegotiate, 7
Number Format, 18

O

Opening workbooks and worksheets
    how to, *9*
Operator symbols in Excel, *12*
Overtime premiums
    amount of premium, 32
    types, 31

P

Page Setup functions, 78
Part-time employees, 26
Paste Special command, 79
    when to use, 47
Pasting cells
    how to, *14*
Pay for non-work time
    types, 39
Percent
    how to format, 34
Percent increase
    union proposal #1, 66
Personal days, 41
PHrs
    named cell, 30

Premium payments
    6th or 7th consecutive day, 36
    call-in, call-out, 36
    holiday worked premiums, 36
    skill-based, 37
    types, 36
Presumptively relevant information, 8
Print gridlines and headlines, 78
Print titles function
    column and row headings, 78
Printing Excel pages, 78
Probationary employees, 20
Productive hours
    change in new contract, 90
    defined, 7

R

Red circled employees, 25
Redo icon. *See* Formatting tools
Referencing cells
    how to, 29, 30
Requesting data from the employer, 7
    sample letter, 92
Retirement plans
    types, 56
RMC FOLDER
    on CD, 4
RMC proposal #1, 75
    flat wage and increment increase, 76
    health insurance, 78
    shift differentials, 80
    summary, 83
    vacations, 82
    wage and increment summary, 77
RMC proposal #2, 87
RMC Workbook
    on CD, 4
RMC Worksheet #1a, 15
RMC Worksheet #1b, 16
RMC Worksheet #1c, 18
RMC Worksheet #2, 23
RMC Worksheet #3, 29
RMC Worksheet #4, 33, 36, 38
RMC Worksheet #5
    holidays, 41
    personal days, 41
    sick leave, 42
RMC Worksheet #6, 46
RMC Worksheet #6a, 47
RMC Worksheet #7
    Health insurance, 51
    life insurance, 55
RMC Worksheet #8, 59
RMC Worksheet #9, 63
Roll-up benefits
    defined, 61

Roll-up factor
    defined, 62

S

Seniority creep
    step progression, 67
    vacation eligibility, 70
Severance pay, 43
Shift differentials
    flat, 33
    percent, 34
Short-term disability insurance, 48, 54
    self-insured employers, 54
Show All Comments tool
    how to use, 34
Sick leave, 42
Sickness and accident insurance (S&A benefits), 54
Step advancement, 67
SUM mathematical operator (=SUM), 15
Supplemental unemployment benefits (SUB), 56
Symmetrical block of columns
    retaining formulas, 79

T

Tab split bar
    how to use, 29
Tabs
    viewing more worksheets. *See* Opening workbooks and worksheets
Text Format, 18
Total Annual Cost
    defined, 6
TotEmp
    named cell, 28
Tuition allowance, 56, 58

U

Undo icon. *See* Formatting tools
Unhide rows and columns
    how to, 38
Uniform allowance, 56
Union business leave, 43
Union proposal #1, 65
    health insurance, 72
    holidays and personal days, 69
    increment and percent wage increase, 65
    longevity pay, 73
    step advancement, 67
    summary, 74
    vacations, 70
    wage and increment increase, 68
Union proposal #2, 84
    health insurance, 85

Union Proposal #2
　shift differentials, 85
　wages, 85

V

Vacations
　eligibility periods, 44
　pay rates, 45
　pro-rata benefits, 46

Viewing formulas
　Ctrl + tilde ~ key, 16

W

Warning and error messages, 35
Weighted average, *11*
Wrap Text
　how to, 19

Acknowledgements

This book is dedicated to my father and mother. To my father Mark for taking me to the union hall during his biennial strikes in the 1950s and giving me my first taste of unionism as well as for teaching me that working hard and doing tasks carefully are good qualities. To my mother Ruth for encouraging academic pursuits and for always supporting me no matter how strange or nonsensical some of my choices may have seemed.

To the thousands of dedicated unionists I had the opportunity to associate with – at the negotiating table, on picket lines and at rallies, and learning together in classrooms as well as barrooms – thank you.

To elected union leaders at all levels who gave me the opportunity to contribute to building stronger unions, thank you for your confidence. Special thanks to the George Meany Center for Labor Studies for allowing me to broaden my knowledge and skills within its halls both as a student and as a staff member.

I thank Lynne Mingarelli of the American Federation of Teachers for initiating the training programs that led to the subsequent preparation of this manual and for allowing data from AFT contracts to be used as the basis of the RMC workbook.

Jeff MacDonald of the Air Line Pilots Association and my mentor at the George Meany Center provided cogent comments on costing methodology. Lynn Feekin of the Labor Education and Research Center, University of Oregon thoroughly edited the manuscript and field-tested the Excel workbooks. Their assistance was invaluable and is most appreciated.

Any errors, large or small, are my responsibility alone – DS

About the author

Donald Spatz was a staff member with the International Union of Electrical, Radio and Machine Workers, the United Cement, Lime and Gypsum Workers International Union, and the International Brotherhood of Boilermakers, Iron Ship Builders, Blacksmiths, Forgers and Helpers. Throughout the 1970s and 1980s he was active in leading contract negotiations and planning and executing contract campaigns as well as developing union training programs and furthering workplace health and safety initiatives.

In 1991 he joined the staff of the AFL-CIO's George Meany Center for Labor Studies/National Labor College as a Senior Staff Associate, teaching classes in contract negotiations, leadership development, contract campaigns, strategic planning, organizing, and teaching techniques. He worked directly with many national and international unions in designing and teaching programs for their union leaders as well as with the American Center for International Labor Solidarity in Bosnia and Herzegovina and other countries of central and southeastern Europe.

He currently lives in Bratislava, Slovakia with his wife Lucia. He can be contacted at spatz.donald@gmail.com.